# JOURNALISM
## — FOR —
# BEGINNERS

# JOAN CLAYTON

# JOURNALISM
## FOR
## BEGINNERS

### How to get into print and get paid for it

PIATKUS

Dedicated to Stan Nicholls,
A great pal
A great help.

First published 1992 by Judy Piatkus (Publishers) Ltd,
5 Windmill Street, London W1P 1HF

**The moral right of the author has been asserted**

*A catalogue record for this book is available
from the British Library*

ISBN 0 7499 1188 3

Designed by Chris Warner

Typeset in Great Britain by
Phoenix Photosetting Ltd, Chatham, Kent
Printed and bound in Great Britain by
Butler & Tanner Ltd, Frome and London

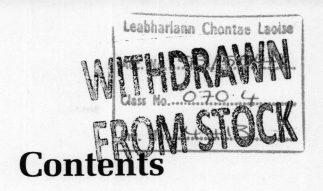
# Contents

# Turning Professional

This book is based on the intensive *Journalism for Beginners* classes I run for Westminster Council Adult Education Colleges in London. On average, twenty per cent of my students are in print by the end of the twelve-week course.

The classes have a reputation for their hard-nosed, professional approach. Students on one course alone were published in the *Observer*, *Daily Mail*, *London Evening Standard* and *Ireland's Own* newspapers, plus *Best* and *Time Out* magazines. And one landed a job on a local paper.

I want to help you get into print and be paid for it.

Armed with the skills learned from this book, you will have plenty of choice. You can freelance and/or confidently apply for a job as a trainee reporter on a newspaper, a trade or industrial tabloid, or local radio station.

I'm not an academic with nothing but theoretical textbook knowledge to offer you. For years I've worked on the staff of various newspapers and magazines.

I now freelance. I produce publications for industry – my current clients are in executive recruitment, pharmaceuticals, oil and the employment of severely disabled people. I also write for the consumer press and national newspapers.

Writing – journalism in particular – is my whole life. And so far it's been a tremendous life – I'd do it all over again. Journalism pays my mortgage. I think it's great that people are willing to give me money for something I started as a hobby.

Wearing my editor's hat, I'm going to tell you how things look from that side of the desk. I outline what editors want from writers and what they don't want.

Anyone reading this merely for the glamour of journalism and

1

because they think it's an easy career option, had better think again. Journalism is hell on wheels. Yes, the magnetism, fascination, excitement, challenge, money, fame and tremendous job satisfaction are certainly all there. But only if you develop a professional approach, have determination and stamina and are prepared to work your socks off.

Joan Clayton
London

# Chapter 1

# Why Do Journalists Write?

- Market research first, writing comes second
- Saleable topics
- What do you want to write, and why?

- Journalism is a technique, it can be learned
- Who makes the rules?

---

'MOST of the good writing in this country is journalism. Journalism is attractive, it will make you immediate money – and you can go on into radio and TV.'

ALAN COREN, Editor, *Punch* and *The Listener*

---

**F**IRST, I'd like you to focus on WHY you want to be a journalist – WHY you're reading this book. What I'm going to say is not just an academic introduction. It's the concept that spells the difference between a journalist's success and failure.

## Why do journalists write?

Notice I say journalists, not people. Everyone who's literate writes – letters, diaries, shopping lists, you name it. But YOU want to learn to be a journalist. Why DO YOU want to write? Perhaps to rant about an injustice, to focus on a social issue, or eulogise a new discovery that will benefit mankind? Or to provide some insight into the private persona of a public figure?

The world and his wife, scribbling about these topics in their diaries and letters, write *subjectively*. But that isn't the way journalism works. Journalists write *objectively* with an audience in mind – the general public.

The first thing to realise is that all creative people are lost without an audience. How effective is a person who plays Hamlet only to his bedroom mirror? And closet scribblers – how influential are they if they restrict themselves to private diaries? Neither is worthy of the name actor or writer.

The professional writing process is not complete until the work has found a readership.

To be successful a writer must be read by others. Yes, that's extremely basic – but too many would-be journalists live in blinkers. They see only the first part of the process – the writing. They fail to see the second part – *getting it read*.

Printed journalism has a two-fold benefit – the reader learns something new; the writer gets paid.

*Question*: How does the journalist reach the reader?
*Answer*: They get work published.
*Question*: What sort of writing is published?
*Answer*: Only what readers want to read.

Remember, newspapers and magazines are SOLD – people won't pay money for what doesn't interest them.

Which brings us to basics. What do the general public want to read? Why do you as a reader, buy any publication? Your daily newspaper for example, what do you expect from it? Ask your friends – what do they expect from their newspaper? Ask lots of people. THEY are the readers who buy the newspapers. Note down their answers: that's what they want to read – that's what they want YOU to write    People read

(1) to be informed,
(2) to be entertained.

Using an entertaining, original style to write up information will be what gets your work accepted by editors. That's part of the creative mainspring of journalism. Don't let anyone tell you journalism isn't creative.

If you've learned nothing else so far, you've still got value for money if you've taken on board the fact that no journalist writes in a vacuum. All work is written with a reader firmly in mind.

## Market research first, writing comes second

You should NEVER write a feature, THEN look for a publication you hope will take it. The logical sequence, if you want to be read, is that you FIRST identify the readership before ever putting your pen to paper.

You may not be fully appreciating what I'm telling you – so I'll repeat it in different terms. Writing is only half the battle to become a professional journalist. Just as big a job is SELLING your piece to an editor.

This book is about how to become a journalist. *You're not a journalist till you regularly have your work in print.*

And I'll tell you how, of course.

## Saleable topics

One example of an ideally saleable topic is injustice. This motivates many successful journalists. You can do a great service to yourself and possibly humanity at large if you get your protests to the reading public. And I mean as a piece of journalism, NOT a letter to the editor. That, again, is subjective, merely a whinge in disguise. Your printed words (handled the right way) can result in some action being taken. You can sway opinion. Never under-estimate the power of the pen.

Each of us nurtures our personal sets of prejudices, assumptions and expectations. This is what gives our views individuality. This applies equally whether you have a drum to beat or aim to write more descriptive pieces such as travelogues.

## What do you want to write and why?

Let's now look at (a) exactly WHAT you want to write, and (b) WHY you want to write it.

Journalists are what are known as ACTIVE writers – as compared with, say essayists. Something HAPPENS as a result of people reading a piece of journalism: readers gain more information on a topic – they LEARN SOMETHING NEW. Please keep that in mind – your piece MUST tell the readers something they didn't know before or it won't get into print.

This maxim applies whatever the subject. Here are a few topics that could be the basis of features people will want to read and editors will want to buy. Possibly your aim is among them:

(1) you want to reveal an injustice in the hope that some action will be taken. Perhaps you've discovered a family who are to be put out of their home because of a bungle at the local council office;
(2) you have a solution to a current problem – perhaps ridding the streets of litter;
(3) you have discovered a fascinating museum that's just opened: you want to describe it to persuade others to visit it;
(4) you want to report a recent news event (eg, the opening of a new sports centre) so that others will be informed;
(5) you've a cause you want to champion or a charity you want to raise funds for;
(6) you want to interview a best-selling author about his or her latest book;
and of course there are many more.

Take a break for a minute. Sit down now and briefly list the subjects you want to write about. This will help you clarify your path towards becoming a journalist.

## Journalism can be learned

About the old adage that writers are born, not made. It's actually a bit of both. What you're born with is an individual way of expressing yourself. This manifests itself as early as before you learn to walk. What you learn at school is syntax, grammar, punctuation and spelling. What you can learn from this book are rules apropos style, angle, length, speed, responsibilities and thinking on your feet. Once understood, these precepts turn a person into a journalist.

The creative part is working within the confines of these

guidelines. All journalists understand these restraints; once you learn them you start on an equal footing with the professionals.

## Who makes the rules?

Now, who do you think lays down journalistic rules?

Not editors.

Most are decreed by the reading public's purse or wallet. Always remember, editors stake their jobs on taking your work. Their expertise is knowing what the readers want.

Now is a lucrative time for freelance journalists who can prove they have a professional approach. Editors have to work to a budget and suffer staff cutbacks the same as any other manager – so they have to use freelances. Editors are more than happy if they discover a *reliable* contributor. (They're also pleased because they don't have to pay them when they're sick or on holiday, neither do they have to fork out for their National Insurance or pension contributions!)

# Chapter 2

# The Professional Approach

- Defining journalism
- Why presentation is important
- What happens to your MS
- How to lay out MSS
- Why exercises are important

---

'WHAT makes the heart sink is the sheer amount of wasted effort by an army of people who submit MSS all over the place with a scattergun effect. Ninety per cent have no relevance.'

ALAN RUSBRIDGER, Features Editor, *Guardian*

---

THE STATESMAN Edmund Burke recognised the immense power of the Press when, in the 1700s, he dubbed it the 'Fourth Estate'. As you know, the other three estates are the Lords, the Commons and the Church. It's surprising that, although journalism's importance has long been recognised by industry, commerce and the general public, it is only in recent years that it's been possible in the UK for journalism to be taken as a degree subject.

Both academically and commercially, journalism as a profession has been a bit of a grey area. It's too often thought of as something the talented just 'do', like the arts. And the idea of 'training' is only vaguely acknowledged. But as with a concert pianist or sculptor, to be a success a journalist needs to train assiduously and develop a *professional approach*. What is meant by that?

Reliability. Consistently high-standard work. On deadline. Always arriving punctually for appointments. ALL facts checked and correct, including places, times, dates and the spelling of names. Work written to specified length. Presented in the most easily and quickly assimilated manner.

Amateurs make editors NERVOUS. Amateurs don't check facts. Then irate readers write in. Editors have even been known to go to jail for libels written by beginner writers. Irresponsible journalists can get editoral staff into all sorts of fertiliser. They only embarrass them once, mind. They never write for that publication again – or possibly any other. Editors are a tight-knit fraternity. They warn each other.

This book isn't written for the 'I think I'd like tos', but for the 'I wills'. If you want to succeed it's VITAL that you develop a professional approach.

## What exactly is journalism?

Let me now give you my definition of journalism. If you're serious about becoming a journalist, you can type it out and pin it on the wall above your desk.

Good journalism is:

(a) *topical;*
(b) *informative;*
(c) *contains quotes,*

*and is written in a concise, interesting style within the confines of a specific number of words.*

The non-journalists, ie the general article writers:

(1) often use long words and sentences to impress with their erudition;
(2) can't fully explore their subject in 1,000 words;
(3) produce non-vivific prose derived entirely from book research and their own experiences. In other words, they do not include topical quotes from people they have recently interviewed.

# Why presentation is important

However good your writing, however original, gripping, amusing, however deep the message: IF YOU PUT OBSTACLES IN THE WAY OF THE EDITOR READING IT, THE PIECE DOESN'T STAND A HOPE.

I wonder if you have ever sabotaged your chances in this way? Remember. You're the SELLER. The editor is the buyer. You've got a big persuasion job. And you're NOT THERE PERSONALLY TO DO IT. Your work stands naked and alone. The editor assesses it on a number of pointers – the first being 'Can I read it?'

# What happens to your MS

Do you see editors as 'the enemy'? Fighting against editors' dictums is what novices do. Successful writers apply psychology. They find out what editors want and WORK WITH THEM. Let me tell you what happens to your typescript.

In comes the morning post. Small magazines receive only half a dozen freelance MSS (manuscripts); on a popular magazine it could be a dozen or so. The *London Evening Standard* gets 200 to 400 a week, *Best* 400.

Because of publishing's supersonic pace the editor's job is controlling one crisis after another. She's constantly frantically busy. Her secretary's trained to stop phone calls and visitors interrupting her work.

This day-after-day pressure means MSS aren't read straight away. Solicited and unsolicited freelance contributions are put into a specific tray. The editor (or whoever's job it is to 'taste copy') will try to tackle this pile of reading at least once a week before it becomes too daunting.

MSS from professionals are different from those of amateurs because established writers are hectically busy themselves and empathise with the editor's problems. Have you ever received a letter you can't read all through because of bad handwriting? Was it time-consuming?

Most editors don't have time to even *attempt* to read handwritten work, even the carefully written ones. Most are put straight in the 'reject' tray unread. I always do that. We don't *want* to. It's merely an inevitability of time pressure.

By the way, there are only three reasons for bad handwriting – intention, arrogance and ignorance. Many doctors used deliberately to write prescriptions illegibly so that patients couldn't deciphere the medication prescribed, and the habit has lingered. That leaves only arrogance and ignorance for authors submitting MSS.

Never send in handwritten work. If you don't have a typewriter, pay a professional typist. Find one in the Yellow Pages, the local paper or the small ads newsagents put in their windows.

The same goes for MSS typed with a worn-out ribbon that's barely legible, or a cheap dot matrix word processor printer. Most American publications state in their directory *Writer's Market* that they won't read anything off a dot matrix printer. Having to peer at something takes up time.

Some journals won't accept pieces typed with single-line spacing because this is more tiring to read than double. It also makes word counting difficult.

Don't knock the editor, she's reading fifty MSS a week and that's about one per cent of her job.

Even if in double-line spacing, MSS can be made difficult to read by other factors such as typing on both side of the page, or on coloured paper (which also doesn't photocopy so well as white). Crossings-out and penned notes are additional reading problems for editorial staff.

Mark this too – editors hate text with a right-hand margin that's JUSTIFIED (where all the last words in the line end at exactly the same place). It may look smart at first glance, but it creates unnatural and confusing spaces between and within words. It makes the calculation of the number of words more difficult. Don't do it. Justify the left-hand margin only.

I'm afraid these gaffes identify the writer as an amateur immediately. As with any trade, craft or profession the potential buyer (editor) thinks: 'This vendor doesn't even know the basics. if they haven't taken the trouble to find out, their writing's probably slipshod too.' So the would-be journalist is batting on a losing wicket as soon as the MS is taken out of the envelope.

These aren't arrogant rules dreamed up by editors and publishers. They're the BASICS OF COMMUNICATING. *You* understand the piece – you've lived with it for days, weeks even – but your recipient comes to it cold. He needs help, not the hindrance of obscurity, and careless writing or typing. It's difficult enough to get into print; competition is fierce out there. It's pointless reducing your chances even further.

Editors don't retype MSS.

To learn on, get a second-hand manual typewriter. They're quite cheap in the classified ads. Look upon it as a good investment. Typing lessons are available cheaply at evening classes.

But when you've got touch typing under your belt march with the technocrats. Invest in a word processor. Today's journalism is too fiercely competitive to be able to survive without one. On a WP you can do twenty re-drafts in the same time as it takes to do just one on a typewriter.

And the writing's on the wall that most editors will eventually accept pieces *only on disc*, not hard copy (words on paper).

## This is how a professional lays out an MS

(1) Always type on one side of white, A4 size paper;

(2) *top of 1st page* – (on the right) author's name, address, telephone and fax numbers;
(then, beneath it, on the left) number of words, plus serial rights offered: FBSR, 2nd BSR, N.Am.SR, etc (see Chapter 25 on Serial Rights);
(then, beneath it, centre) title plus your by-line to establish whether you're using a pseudonym or not;

(3) margins always 1½ inches all round (for printer's marks);

(4) never justify right-hand margins, always justify the left;

(5) indent all paragraphs (you're not setting out a letter);

(6) double-line spacing;

(7) number all pages at *top right*;

(8) *bottom right* always type 'MORE';

(9) at finish, in centre, always type 'ENDS'.

## Exercises are to help you

At the learning stage the only way you can accurately and usefully assess your progress and level of commitment to becoming a journalist is by doing the exercises in this book. They are not merely academic. They are always complete, or parts of, news reports, features, profiles or reviews.

Self-motivation is an essential part of a writer's combat equipment. If you only do the exercises because of guilt, then you haven't the right attitude towards becoming a journalist.

## Chapter 3

# Getting Ideas

- Ideas book
- Cuttings files
- Radio and TV
- Letters to the editor and agony columns

- Anniversaries
- Exercise 1 – CIPP/CIS
- Angles
- Exercise 2

'WITH ideas you have to be disciplined. Lots of people have ideas, but not many can deliver them. That's what makes a good journalist.'

SALLY O'SULLIVAN, Editor, *Harpers & Queen*

OPPORTUNITIES for journalists are far greater than those for short story writers. Publications print at least four times as much non-fiction as fiction.

If saleable non-fiction ideas don't come easily to you, there are many ways of originating them. After a while you'll find they'll be triggered by incidents that happen to you, events you'll read about in a newspaper or magazine, see on the box, a chance comment in a conversation. But for now, let me give you a number of sources.

## Ideas book

Never move without a small notebook because loose scraps of paper tend to get lost. Whenever you get even a smidgen of an idea, note it down. You'll gradually build up a collection of all sorts of ideas, angles, phrases, and information sources, and they'll be useful at some time. All professionals have well-worn ideas books.

# Cuttings files

Build up files of press cuttings on topics that interest you. Add to these the notes you take from your coverage of radio or TV programmes. This way you have up-to-date facts on your chosen subjects.

One of the reasons a newspaper can produce features at speed is because it has vast files of clips from its own and other newspapers on every topic that's ever seen print. All professional journalists have stacks of A4 size envelopes or files crammed with cuttings.

Make a separate envelope for each subject, each clearly labelled in capital letters.

You'll start sub-dividing too. You might start a file on, say, 'Mugging'. As you collect clips you'll find it more convenient to start fresh envelopes for a series of cuttings on 'Mugging Old Ladies' and 'Gay-bashing' – with perhaps another on 'Victim Support Groups'.

Eventually you may specialise, but at the start collect everything on anything that remotely interests you. Then, next time the news breaks on that topic, you'll be prepared to write a feature on it. Don't restrict your horizons.

Valuable tip – ALWAYS REMEMBER to write on every cutting two things:

(a)  the title of the publication from which it came,
(b)  the date it was printed.

Those two are vital. The date helps when you're writing a feature which includes background details with step-by-step chronological developments.

And you'll sometimes want more information. So you'll need to phone the publication which printed the clip. As this could be days, weeks or even months later, they often can't help you unless you can help them find the piece. They'll need you to tell them, for example: 'It's on page five of your 20th October edition under the heading "People Without a Country".' Then they will be able to go to their files and find background details relevant to that particular piece.

Again, your piece isn't top standard journalism unless you can include quotes. They add spice and credibility. You could be writing about, say, London's homeless. Your piece has extra weight if you can write: 'In the *Independent* last week Malcolm Smith interviewed the Social Services Minister who said: "£2 million has been allocated to deal with this problem"'. You couldn't write this unless, on your cutting, you'd noted the publication, plus the date.

Albert Einstein said something along the lines that he didn't clutter up his brain with remembering facts as he needed it for creative thinking. Journalists work on the same principle. *They don't need to know a lot about any subject. All they need to know is where to go for the information.* The first step is your cuttings file.

Just one example of a saleable feature where clips are invaluable is the seven-day-wonder. Something spectacular happens – an air crash, hurricane, mass murder or fire. When it occurs, the professional journalist is *thinking ahead*. Would a follow-up make a good feature? Readers will be interested in the repercussions six months or one year later. So you'd collect all the current cuttings on that particular disaster.

# Radio and TV

Radio and TV are great sources for ideas. Among the best spots are phone-ins; and particularly news and magazine programmes. One of my private students had five pieces published that he developed from ideas he heard on *Woman's Hour*.

Don't think because you're male you can't make plenty of money writing for women's magazines. It's the *biggest* market there is and therefore *needs the most material from freelances*. (I cover the women's market in Chapter 19.)

*Punters* on Radio 4 is another good programme for saleable ideas, also spots such as *Any Questions*, the BBC 1 TV *Them and Us*, and *Call Nick Ross*.

# Letters to the editor and agony columns

These are surprisingly rich sources for those who want to write the 'social consciousness' pieces that are very popular with editors. Read the letters and agony columns in all the newspapers and magazines you can get hold of. You'll find plenty of original opinions on current issues.

For work to have a balanced viewpoint it's vital to get quotes from a number of people, both to support your idea and giving the opposite viewpoint. And there you have a saleable feature.

# Anniversaries

Many journalists earn a regular income from writing anniversary commemorations. There are several notable anniversaries on every day of the year, so you're never short of ideas. The piece has the greatest chance of acceptance if you *start with an incident happening today* in that connection. Although an anniversary is a historical event, readers still want something NEW about it.

**Example introduction:** 'Robert Peary would joyfully have eaten his snow shoes if he could have seen the latest sub-zero camping equipment invented by leading researchers. Arctic explorer Peary was the first man to reach the North Pole – he died 70 years ago today.'

**Example intro:** 'Today sees the arrival of the first youngster at a new type of training centre for school leavers. It was five years ago today that teenager Steven Smith made history by being the first almost totally paralysed person to land a job as a computer programmer. He showed by example that disabled people are an untapped source of skill. The Government made a grant to set up a training centre for disabled people who can make a significant contribution to industry.'

The above examples are hypothetical, of course, but invaluable anniversaries are listed in *The Writers' & Artists' Yearbook*, Events of the Year are listed in *Whitaker's Almanack*. Another source is

*Pears Cyclopaedia* – look under Chronicle of Events – also *Dates &
Events* by Everyman and *20th Century Chronicles*.

Naturally, the other source is your cuttings files.

# Ears

Keep them open. A journalist is a listening camera – a keen
observer. Chance remarks overheard often spark ideas. Note them
in your ideas book.

## EXERCISE 1

*CIPP (Create Ideas from People and Problems)* is a method of
lateral thinking that never fails to help. This is a lesson in how to
control the despair when a piece of blank paper remains blank.

All journalists without exception experience writer's cramp –
not of hand, but of brain. These mental blocks visit the experienced and inexperienced. When this happens to a professional
who won't be able to pay the rent if she doesn't sell something this
week, she can't wait for the block to disperse. She has to do
something positive immediately.

CIPP gives you the outline of a saleable idea from one word. It
will also give you the best angle, which helps select the market.
Dedicated learner journalists will never let a day pass without
coming up with at least one saleable idea (even if they don't write it
up straight away). The more you practise, the better you get.

There's nothing difficult about CIPP. Any number can play. In
fact, input from other people can be very helpful, and they don't
have to be writers. You may already use this system, or something
similar.

You start by writing down a subject. Then you add anything
connected with it that your stream of consciousness comes up
with. This method gives feature writers a choice of avenues so they
can explore the most interesting.

You need a pen, lots of A4 size paper (not a small notebook; A3
size paper is even better). Your cuttings files and ideas book are
useful sources to get CIPP started.

For the first one, follow the chart opposite.

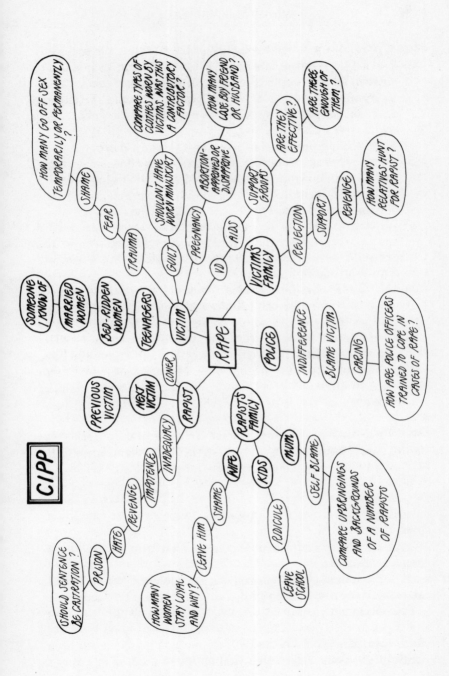

(1) Write the SUBJECT in the centre of the page – circle it.

(2) Journalism is essentially about PEOPLE. Around your subject, write in all the people connected with it – circle them.

(3) Everyone has PROBLEMS. What headaches could the subject cause the people? Write problems near the person; link each to the person with a line.

(4) Keep adding problems till you can't think of more.

(5) Let your stream of consciousness flow – write down everything that comes into your head connected with what's in the centre of the page, including possible solutions to problems. At least one line should reveal a saleable ANGLE to pursue.

(6) When you have an idea/angle beginning to emerge, take a fresh sheet of A4 paper. Write the developing idea in the centre. You now have the space to expand it into a working outline/structure for a feature.

(7) CIS (*Create Ideas from a Subject*) is merely a more basic form of CIPP. If you really can't find an idea in your ideas book or cuttings files, use CIS before going on to CIPP. Write a single word (a noun) in the centre of your page. Write around it all its component parts. Then write down all the thoughts you have on each of them. Try it right now. Note down the first noun you can think of. Try 'house', or 'tree' (see my example opposite).

When you have a positive theme emerging, take a fresh sheet of paper, write on it the nucleus of the thought and apply CIPP to develop it into an outline for your piece.

# Angles

By the way, here's a little more definition on ANGLE. *It's a specific aspect of a subject.*

No editor would take a general piece on violence. Why? Because masses has been written on it. But an editor would be interested in a new ANGLE on violence.

**Example:** This could be an UPDATE piece on people in the aftermath of an attack, say. Some victims spend months in hospital,

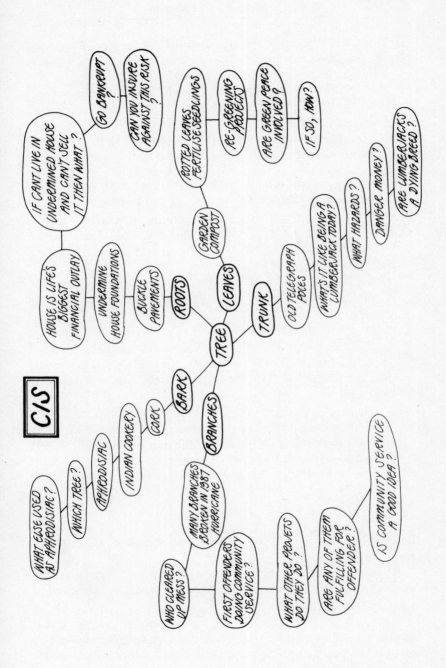

C/S

WHAT ELSE USED AS APHRODISIAC?

WHICH TREE?

APHRODISIAC

INDIAN COOKERY

CORK

BARK

ROOTS

BUCKLE PAVEMENTS

UNDERMINE HOUSE FOUNDATIONS

HOUSE IS LIFE'S BIGGEST FINANCIAL OUTLAY

IF CAN'T LIVE IN UNDERMINED HOUSE AND CAN'T SELL IT THEN WHAT?

GO BANKRUPT?

CAN YOU INSURE AGAINST THIS RISK?

ROTTED LEAVES FERTILISE SEEDLINGS

RE-GREENING PROJECTS

ARE GREEN/PEACE INVOLVED?

IF SO, HOW?

GARDEN COMPOST

LEAVES

TREE

TRUNK

OLD TELEGRAPH POLES

WHAT'S IT LIKE BEING A LUMBERJACK TODAY?

WHAT HAZARDS?

DANGER MONEY?

ARE LUMBERJACKS A DYING BREED?

BRANCHES

MANY BRANCHES BROKEN IN 1987 HURRICANE

WHO CLEARED UP MESS?

FIRST OFFENDERS DOING COMMUNITY SERVICE

WHAT OTHER PERVERTS DO THEY DO?

ARE ANY OF THEM FULFILLING FOR OFFENDER?

IS COMMUNITY SERVICE A GOOD IDEA?

some develop phobias which can affect their job and or personal relationships.

**Example:** Another angle on violence could be the current position of battered grannies (elderly parents abused by their own family);

**Example:** Yet another – a survey of new support groups set up in a particular area.

Those are all specific aspects of violence – they're all ANGLES.
Or we could look at something that's front page news.

**Example:** You ring the news editor of a national to say you have a story on yesterday's London train crash. Because his staff have covered it in full he'll yawn and start to hang up on you. But before he does you say: 'I've got a new angle.'
He'll ask: 'What is it?'
You say: 'I've interviewed one of the passengers who is in hospital. Last time she was in hospital was as a result of the Birmingham train disaster only six months ago. I've got some good quotes.'
Chances are he'll then be interested because you've an original angle on a current topic.

The criteria for all angles:

(1) Ultra-interesting topic – something people will spend money on a newspaper or magazine to read about.
(2) You *must* have something NEW to say about this topic.

## EXERCISE 2

Think up an idea, in other words an ANGLE, for a saleable feature.
But before you work on your idea, get hold of a copy of the publication you're aiming it at. If you don't already have a subject and an angle, I'd like you to use CIPP and CIS to find it. By the way, don't ever throw away your graphs. You never know when they may come in useful, as topics recur over and over again.
Use the *Writers' & Artists' Yearbook* and *The Writer's Handbook* to help you decide which publication you want to write for. You'll find them in your public library.

# Chapter 4

# News Reporting

- Facts, not opinions
- Formula writing
- By-lines
- Multiple sales
- Local Press
- Speed
- Means of delivery

- Deadlines
- Some jargon: story, copy, editorial, sub-editor
- Responsibility for repercussions

> 'JOURNALISM shouldn't be crusading, putting MY opinion across. Why should my view matter more than Mrs Joe Soap's? A good column should express what READERS are thinking. It should talk about what readers talk about – and in a way they talk about them. I'm a born communicator.'
>
> JEAN ROOK, Columnist, *Sunday Express*

WE'RE NOW getting closer to the action – the writing. We've discussed what you want to write and why. We've also covered various methods of finding ideas and angles, plus defining exactly what an angle is. I hope you did the exercises.

In Chapter 5 you're going to write a couple of news stories. In this chapter I'll tell you how – I'm going to cover news reporting in depth.

News reporting is what's known as *pure journalism*. It's the original factual communication, the style you'll find in all your newspapers. *It's the basis of all pungent non-fiction with impact published for today's readership*. This is the SPADEWORK. Learn it, and you'll have no difficulty in writing the saleable news features, profiles and reviews covered later in this book. Specialise in it, and you can legitimately apply for a job on a local newspaper or on your local radio station.

News reporting is FACTS – FACTS – repeat FACTS. It's never OPINION. Never assumption. Keep *yourself* out of it. That comes later when an editor asks you to become a Special Correspondent or when you are writing reviews. For now, you write like all the other thousands of newspaper reporters. Remember, you are a camera. Go and observe. Report the facts you see – nothing more. No embroidery, that's the mark of the amateur.

Never overestimate the readers' knowledge, never underestimate their intellect. Give the general public the truth and let their integrity do the rest.

And you have a responsibility to posterity to be rigidly factual. Journalists have a dual role in that they are also recorders of history. In 50 or 100 years' time people will read your news story or feature in the newspaper library.

I read a very pertinent letter in an issue of *Journalist's Week* from Jean Silvan Evans, Senior Lecturer in journalism at the University of Wales.

She was answering a letter from a journalism student who asked: 'Why should journalists preserve a distance between themselves and their subjects, especially when their real feelings are far from impartial?' Jean Silvan Evans gave me permission to reprint her reply here:

Few publishers would launch a newspaper or magazine in the eager hope that the reading public was waiting for the views and opinions of young people inexperienced in life and journalism on all the urgent topics of the day, from the ozone layer to the Poll Tax.

Yet some young people seeking to become journalists seem to believe the whole publishing industry was set up as a vehicle to channel their own comments to the world.

Without getting into how many facts can dance on the point of a needle, the answer is that FACTS ARE GREATER THAN OPINIONS. And facts are what journalism, at bottom and at best, is all about.

Experienced journalists are not eager to judge. It is not their first duty. Journalists should seek to be the eyes and ears of their readers – not their minds. Given the facts, readers are well able to judge for themselves.

Good journalists develop a respect for the people they write for and about.

Harold Evans put it precisely in the memorial service of journalist David Blundy, killed by a random bullet while covering El Salvador for *The Sunday Correspondent*. After he had filed his story, David went back to the barrio to 'write the last par'. There was just a chance the material gathered for the last par might affect his story's balance. And to him, 'that was all that mattered', he said.

People who do not, first, realise the power and predominance of facts are rarely likely to have any comment worth considering. Young people cannot turn themselves into Duncan Campbells and Paul Foots without the tireless research and commitment to facts that entails.

As well as saying comment was free but facts were sacred, C.P. Scott might have added that comment based on the sacredness of facts was expensive. People with a reputation in any area do not lightly rush into conclusions or print. Time, energy, research, judgement and vision, have to be paid for.

Why should young people expect that just being a journalist (rather than a lawyer or engineer) should elevate their view of life above that of their, usually, far more experienced readers? To seek to thrust them on readers is presumptuous, arrogant and intrusive.

It is also unprofitable.

Journalism is a complex and sophisticated calling that demands the skills of the surgeon, not the butcher. When society depends for its knowledge of itself on journalists, these skills must be well-honed. The more direct route of the butcher can only damage people's trust in journalists. It also betrays the high calling of journalists to serve society as its messengers.

And ethical questions are an integral, not an add-on, part of journalism and are addressed with every story written. Far from being uncharted, the ethical territory for the student journalist is charted clearly between the compass points of accuracy, honesty, judgement and integrity.

Far from being 'irrelevant and impractical' when putting words on a page, that is the only time these qualities can be put to the test.

# Formula writing

Study the news pages of different newspapers. You'll notice that most of the pieces could have been written by the same person. Why? Because news reporting is FORMULA writing.

Local correspondents are the bread and butter of the regional and provincial papers. Study your local paper, and write for it whether or not you're planning to apply for a job with them. This style is the criterion all editors use for staff writers and for free-lances. You won't make a fortune writing for the local Press, but it *is* paid and it's the best free apprenticeship you can have.

# By-lines

It's also a good source of by-lines. By-line is jargon for the author's acknowledgement – 'By Mary Smith' – printed on the page at the beginning or the end of a piece. Often, for short news items, only staff writers get by-lines, but you should get one if you have a news feature accepted. By-lines are valuable. They're your collateral when submitting work to editors. They will ask to see cuttings of what you've had printed because they want to see the quality of your work.

Apart from needing by-lines to prove credibility, the artistic creator's need for recognition is surely justified? By-lines in one form or other aren't new. Painters and sculptors often sign their work. Just one among many – I'm particularly intrigued by a wood carver's 'by-line'. Paycocke's is a house built in 1505, in Coggeshall, Essex. On the hall's timbered ceiling are carved flor-ets. All except one, which is an acorn-size likeness of the craftsman.

The more news stories you get accepted by your local paper, the more you'll develop a 'nose for news', a 'nose for an angle'.

Good standard news stories are as succint as possible. You won't find padding. Once you've learned to write with a rigid economy of words editors will be interested in your work. The style opens all sorts of doors to news features for national Press and radio, to news magazines, to syndicated work.

# Multiple sales

Look ahead – plan for AFTER you've written the news story. You can get a lot of mileage from a single item. No professional sells a good idea only once. Apart from a news story, you can probably get two or more features out of it. It depends on how many angles you can come up with. Remember, you have various categories of publications at which you can aim different angles – dailies, weeklies, monthlies and quarterlies. It's quite legitimate to offer the same story to one of each of these as they're not rivals in readerships. But, of course, each will need to have a different ANGLE on whatever topic the piece is about. They can't be the same unaltered piece.

A private student of mine discovered a woman tiger trainer. He wrote it up as either a news story or news feature from four different angles and sold it to *Chat*, *She*, *Dorset World*, and a local radio programme.

Being a weekly publication, *Chat* is not in competition with any of the other titles. *She* is a monthly and *Dorset World* a quarterly. Radio is altogether a different medium from print. None of these is seriously competing with the others.

The four angles my student came up with were:

(1) for *Best* – do training methods involve cruelty? plus comments from the RSPCA.
(2) for *She* – a female tiger trainer is unique. The focus was on being a woman in the profession, how she coped being also a wife and mother.
(3) for *Dorset World* – the trainer is based in Dorest and was also born there.
(4) for radio – the stress of being constantly packing up, moving on and appearing in a new town. The effects this has on a trainer's family life – and on the tigers.

# Local Press

Back to news reporting – read as many local papers as you can get hold of. Keep them all for future reference. Make a separate file for each title. Note the subjects they cover so you'll know what they accept. In this context, plagiarism is par for the course.

The types of *local* topics that make short NEWS ITEMS/NEWS STORIES are fires, weddings, concerts, festivals, openings of shops and services, closings, improvements, local community and residents' problems and triumphs.

What local topics could make a NEWS FEATURE?

Any of those for news stories (written in depth, of course), plus, say, the problems of buying a flat in the area, finding a creche, raising money for the local hospital or charity. You must be able to think of many more.

And don't forget the local free newspapers. OK, so they don't pay much, if at all, but it's all experience, and you get a bonus if they give you a by-line.

If you live in the capital, remember to analyse copies of the London *Evening Standard*. It comes out 261 times each year. Think of the enormous amount of copy needed to fill it. The *Standard* isn't as parochial as other locals, so don't send it 'regional trivia'. It's closer to being a national (something like the *Manchester Guardian* which eventually became the *Guardian*).

Can you see yourself writing for the local Press? Thousands of would-be journalists start on their own town paper.

# Speed – how it affects the writer

Freelances and potential staff reporters need to be aware of the frantic SPEED at which a newspaper operates; *any* newspaper, be it local or national. Editors are constantly making split-second decisions on their feet as stories come in by phone and fax. Staff reporters have to be able to immediately break into a gallop to get to the fire, murder, or whatever in the shortest possible time and get the story back to the editor.

The speed is exciting. Addictive. It triggers the adrenalin. I work best under pressure. Most journalists do. If they can't stand the heat, they get out of the kitchen. Public Relations is full of failed journalists.

I remember a student saying: 'But Public Relations pays better.' That's not the case. Salaries in PR and journalism vary as widely as in any other field. But even if it were, let's take another couple of comparisons. Strip clubs often pay their dancers more than the Royal Ballet. You can make more money writing porn than a gardening column.

## The editor needs it – fast

If you're freelancing for a newspaper, getting copy to them fast can be tricky. Today's postal service leaves much to be desired. First class post no longer guarantees following-working-day delivery. Even Special Delivery post isn't guaranteed to deliver the next day. Datapost is, but it's expensive; and it still doesn't get there until 24 hours later. If you're only hours away from the deadline your alternatives are: motorbike courier, fax, telex or feet.

I always take it myself if I'm not working concurrently on two projects with deadlines close to one another.

Otherwise there are plenty of fax (facsimile) bureaux. The more professional freelances already have their own fax machines at home. There are something like two dozen models on the market, and at widely varying prices.

But beware of the cheaper ones – you get what you pay for. You need a machine that will spew out perfectly legible copy in the editor's office; if he has to keep asking you to re-transmit, you won't be very popular (see Chapter 26 on technology).

If you work in an office that has a telex, that's another good method.

Keep a note of all local and national newspaper telephone, telex and fax numbers. Papers will take only commissioned stories over the phone – and those rarely. These days they seldom employ copytakers.

Another point to bear in mind is that gradually, more and more editors are accepting copy only on floppy discs instead of hard copy (text on paper). To compete in tomorrow's journalistic arena you need to invest in a home computer/word processor.

A plus point, of course, is that you get paid more. You get whatever is their going rate for the number of words you've written, plus an extra fee because, having the text on disc cuts out their having to set type from hard copy. Make sure you mention this when you discuss payment. By the way, they return the disc to you (well, in theory they do).

# Deadlines

A point also on another aspect of professionalism – DEADLINES. This is something that sorts out the amateurs from the professionals. That editor wants that feature by 10 a.m. Tuesday. In journalism there are as many neurotics, emotional cripples, and alcoholics as anywhere. But despite any personal hangups, copy *must* be on the editor's desk before deadline. Establish a reputation for reliability.

# Jargon

I try to use as little jargon as possible, but there are four more terms you need to know when talking to newspapers and magazines.

1   News reports – what do editors call them? STORIES. Nothing to do with fiction. Divorce them in your mind. An editor sends a reporter to cover a *story*.

2   The reporter writes the story. What are those words on that piece of paper called? COPY. Again, a word with more than one connotation. In publishing a duplicate or *carbon copy* of anything is called just that – dup or carbon or black. The word COPY doesn't mean duplicate, it means anything at all that's to be printed. As well as text it includes photos and artwork.

3   Yet another word with a double meaning is EDITORIAL. This is the old-fashioned name for what today's newspapers call a leader. This is written by either the editor or a leader writer. Both are staffers – full-time employees, that is.

The modern use of EDITORIAL denotes 'the text that isn't advertising copy; which isn't paid for by the advertisers'. In other words, pieces like news stories, features, profiles and reviews written by staffers or freelance journalists.

4   Another word you need to know so you don't get egg on your face is SUB-EDITOR. On no account should you ever confuse a sub with a deputy editor. Subs edit copy, that is, SUBstitute the right words for wrong ones. The sub, not the editor, is the last person who sees the text before it's actually set in type. The editor is a decison-maker. The word SUB-EDITOR describes a job, not a title.

## News reporting – repercussions

Before we actually get down to how to write news reports, a word or two on the aftermath. When writing every story, never forget the effect your words are going to have on people involved in the incident you're covering.

There's also the libel law to worry about, but that's such a vast subject I cover it in Chapter 25.

What I mean here are the harmful psychological effects that can be experienced when an inaccurate news story appears in print. Being the victim of a crime is bad enough – having the incident broadcast by the Press often brings additional problems such as ungrounded accusation, spiteful gossip and being accosted in the street.

So don't lose sight of the dignity and integrity of the person you're interviewing. Always remember that you are speaking to them when they are in shock or in an unnaturally highly emotional state. They will say things they would never say when in a more rational state of mind. And when your piece appears in print, they have to live with the repercussions.

There was an interesting feature on this point by Clifford Singer, a journalism student at Cardiff University. I have permission to reproduce it here:

[Headline] REPORTING VIOLENCE – IT'S A CRIME
[Standfirst] Lots of reporters cover crime just like any other story. But they are talking to people in shock and need much

more sensitivity than on the average industrial round.

[Feature] When Australian-born Bronwen Potts joined the *Bendigo Advertiser* – in a quiet city 90 miles north of Melbourne – she found herself subbing reports about two mass murders.

The reporting of these events became news in itself – accusations of sensationalism led to major government inquiries.

Potts was spurred to examine the complaints for herself. She is now completing her one-year Master's dissertation on the reporting of violence at Cardiff's Centre for Journalism Studies.

Her research involved speaking to editors, police, victims and one mass murderer. She encountered many complaints of inaccuracy. 'A certain amount is forgivable, if it's a sudden incident and there's a need for instant information,' she says. 'But when inaccuracies continue for hours and days – as I was to discover – then there's cause to worry.'

One difficulty results from interviewing people still traumatised by tragedy. Nineteen-year-old ex-army officer cadet Julian Knight shot dead seven people in Clifton Hill. Knight's family and some of his victims lived there, and many witnessed the shoot-out. 'People said things at the time they didn't mean; and that brought flak from the neighbours,' says Potts.

'Lots of reporters cover a crime just like any other story. But they're talking to people in shock and need much more sensitivity than on the average industrial round.'

The second mass murder was when failed law student Frank Vitkovic shot dead eight people then killed himself by jumping from the 11th floor.

'The papers and TV said people were shot in the lifts – which wasn't true,' says Potts. 'But workers who heard the reports were too scared to use the lifts after that.'

Media speculation that the police had unnecessarily barred ambulance people from the building caused the police extra anguish. The coroner later found that they had acted correctly.

Potts believes many inaccuracies could be avoided with

better fact-checking. 'Someone claimed to be the cousin of Julian Knight and made up stories about his family.' They were repeated in the media because nobody bothered to check.

Fierce competition often drives journalists to try to obtain the most sensational story. In the UK, among the tabloids the pressure is just as great.

But she opposed legislation to improve standards. 'It's well within the capacity of the media to fix themselves through better training and their conscience.'

# Chapter 5

# How to Write News Reports

- Who, what, where, when, why, how
- Definition of news
- Start with the result
- Exercise 3
- Story Lead form
- Exercises 4 and 5

---

'JOURNALISTS go to the nationals for money and prestige, then lead a miserable life personally. The real contact with the reader is in the locals. Part of the attraction is the greater satisfaction.'

BRIAN JONES, Editor, *Bristol Evening Post* and ex-Deputy Editor, *The Guardian*

---

THE ETERNAL shortage of staff which plagues local newspapers is your open door as a freelance. So, let me give you the key to becoming a news reporter. This is a trade secret – the formula for writing news stories.

**A**

WHO, WHAT, WHERE, WHEN, WHY, HOW. It's never any different, and it's never incomplete. Unless you have ALL SIX you don't have a classic news story.

**B**

(1) All six facts must be in the first paragraph – in any order.
(2) The first par (paragraph) must consist of no more than two or three sentences.
(3) Sentences, ideally, have a maximum of 27 words.

That's the bedrock of universal journalism.

Why does a formula exist? For a very good reason. It's necessitated by the killing pace at which newspapers are produced.

All subs and page layout artists are trained to cut copy from the bottom up. This rule only works because the journalist sticks to the formula of getting everything into the first paragraph. All subsequent pars qualify it by giving additional information.

Space is always tight – there are so many pieces to cram on each page. In the frantic rush of production, stories are cut WITHOUT BEING READ.

Most stories are cut, whether written by staffers or freelances. Quite often, there's so little space that every par but the first one is ditched. But the editor knows, without having to read it, that because the piece is written to the formula, the full story is there – the who, what, where, when, why, how.

Now do you see why it's imperative to stick rigidly to the formula?

Consequently, no newspaper will accept a news story not written to the formula. It's the criterion of all newspaper editors in the UK and abroad. So, if you've got all the vital facts up in the first couple of sentences, they will know you're a professional.

# Definition

NEWS is exactly what is says it is. Think about it. It's not 'olds', it's 'NEWS'. News stories are never about history. It's vital you discover something new – something that hasn't happened before. That's the main criterion you need for news reporting. Editors are only interested in today and tomorrow, never yesterday.

# Start with the result

When you write up a story you START WITH THE RESULT. Put the RESULT in your opening sentence. It's exactly the opposite to an essay where you work up to the high point.

In news reporting and news features you start straight in with
WHAT HAPPENED THAT'S NEW – what's changed. What's different
now from how things were?

Professionals are never stuck for an opening. They start with the
result. *Action*, a man fired a gun: *result*, someone died. *Action*, a
burglary: *result*, diamond necklace is missing. *Action*, new fertiliser discovered: *result*, roses as large as cabbages. In every case it's
the result you start with.

**Example of an opening to a news story:** 'Roses as large as
cabbages? Yes, they were on show yesterday, exhibited by John
Smith, inventor of new super-fertiliser "Ros-O". He said: "I
experimented at my Winchester nursery for 17 years before I got
the result I wanted."'

In a nutshell, that's the complete story.

Remember, the reader wasn't there. You're a verbal camera –
you're doing a service for those who weren't at the event. Your job
is to observe and use words to pass on the information. A journalist
is a catalyst – the link between the event and the reader.


# EXERCISE 3

To help you write in a professional journalistic style, I want you to
analyse some classic news stories from national and local newspapers. Assessing pieces already in print helps you judge your own
work. All these stories very likely started out approximately 200
words long, but have been cut from the bottom till only this
amount is left.

As in the following example, write across an A4 page the six
essential facts I've already given you – Who, What, Where, When,
Why, How. Then write underneath each the six facts in each story.
I've done the first one for you. The rest are in *Answer 3* at the back
of the book – but you won't learn if you see the answer first. Work
out the other four before you look them up.

'Six police officers were remanded until May 3rd by Bow Street
magistrates yesterday. They were summonsed in relation to a
dispute at Wapping, East London, in 1987.'

*Answer:*

| WHO | WHAT | WHERE | WHEN | WHY | HOW |
|---|---|---|---|---|---|
| Six police officers | were remanded | Bow Street | yesterday | Wapping dispute | by magistrate |

Now analyse the following:

1 'An anti-nuclear protester flew a banner reading "No New Nukes" in a 90-minute demonstration on a 250-ft crane tower in Piccadilly yesterday. Police said the protester, Mr Nigel Trent, of Andover, would not be charged.'

2 'Police in Wolverhampton yesterday set up telephone hotlines for people to give information. They are compiling details about the riot that followed a drugs raid on a pub.'

3 'A new book on Marilyn Monroe could help emotionally disturbed children in Britain. *Marilyn*, published today, reveals that the film star was an emotionally starved woman who was sexually abused as a child.'

4 'Hampstead Crime Prevention Squad is compiling a survey in a bid to identify sex attack danger spots. The area around West End Lane was the scene of 76 sex offences during 1990. It has been identified as a high risk area.'

## Story Lead form

Now, preparatory to writing your own news story, here's another aid. Take a sheet of A4 paper and type out the following STORY LEAD details at the top of the page. You will need as much space below the words as possible. 'Story Lead' and the column of words under it should go as far left as possible, the 'Who to contact' column should go way over on the far right.

| STORY LEAD | WHO TO |
|---|---|
| **Questions:** | CONTACT .......... |
| WHO | JOB TITLE ........... |
| WHAT | ADDRESS ........... |
| WHERE | |
| WHEN | ................... |
| WHY | |
| HOW | PHONE ............. |
| Cost | Date contacted ....... |
| Photo | |

Type it with a good, black ribbon, then use it as a master. Photocopy a supply of blanks so you can use them for news stories, news features, profiles and reviews – in fact any piece of journalism you write. I use them myself. They will give you a helpful structure to work within.

Look at the top right first. Before you even go to the event, fill in the name and details of the person you're to interview. It's vital you SPELL EVERYTHING CORRECTLY – ask them if it's right, they'll be flattered. It could be the name of an eyewitness, say, or owner of a shop that's been burgled.

There are so many traps if you're not careful. Dozens of first and surnames sound the same but can be spelled more than one way: Smith/Smithe/Smyth/Smythe, Patterson/Pattison, Read/Reid, Pierce/Pearce, Davison/Davidson, Thomson/Thompson, Steven/Stephen, May/Mae, Alan/Allen/Alun, Shuan/Sean/Shawn, Eleanor/Elinor, Jane/Jayne, Stuart/Stewart.

On the left are the trigger words of the six facts you must have for a COMPLETE story. After that there's 'cost' which you'll need if it's relevant, then 'photo' to remind you to get one if you think it would enhance your story. Ask your subject if they mind being photographed, or perhaps they have a black and white photo they can let you have.

Under that, well over to the left, write your own trigger words for all the other questions you'll need to ask. Always go to interviews with a list of questions.

# EXERCISE 4

Now, you're going to write a news story. These are the formula guidelines:

(1) Always start with the result.
(2) Never start with the date unless it's significant (eg, an anniversary).
(3) First par never more than 50 words.
(4) Keep pars short – two or three sentences at most.
(5) Aim at a maximum of 25 to 27 words per sentence, never more. Every word must be significant – no padding.
(6) All six essential facts in the first par – WHO, WHAT, WHERE, WHEN, WHY, HOW – in whatever order you like.
(7) The first par must stand up on its own. All subsequent ones justify the first. It must be possible to cut all successive pars but still have the complete story.
(8) Keep the story as brief as possible, use a minimum of adjectives.
(9) Choose short words, not long ones. Always active words, not passive ones. Stress the positive, not the negative.
(10) Stick to facts – no opinions or speculation, that's not the job of the reporter, who is a verbal camera.
(11) Remember the freedom, dignity and rights of the individual – don't violate them.
(12) Bear in mind there's a strict law of libel.

That's how to do it. Now here's an account of an accident. Write it up as a *50-word news story* for an imaginary local newspaper using the formula guidelines. Writing to the exact length is important.

This is all the information you got when you interviewed various people about the incident, including other wedding guests in following cars:

John Smith was invited to his sister's wedding in Whitechester on 18 November. She was to marry a man named Peter who is a Management Consultant.

John is a Computer Programmer. On the day, he travelled alone up the M1 in his Ford Escort. There was a thunderstorm and it poured cats and dogs all the way. He was *probably*, as usual, driving well over the speed limit.

He reached the bridge over the River Swift where the road surface was extra slippery. The car went into a 20-yard skid, plunged through the railings and disappeared under the surface of the water.

The police were called by another car driver who witnessed the incident. While they waited there was no sign of the Ford Escort driver. The police called the fire brigade who dredged the river. They used a crane and grappling hooks to pull out the car. The doors were all firmly locked and the driver dead.

Read through the account a couple of times and select the six essential factors. Write them on your Story Lead Form, exactly as you did when you analysed those printed news stories: this gives you a structure to work within. Write the story in the space beneath them. Don't try to be clever – write it 'straight' – this is FORMULA writing. I give this to my students in class – they usually complete it in 15 minutes.

There are many correct ways of writing up this story. I'd get 25 versions in my class and they'd all be right. At the back of the book you'll find one version in *Answer 4*. But write up your own before you turn to it. If you have more than 50 words, or have omitted any of the six essential factors, then you haven't got it right.

## EXERCISE 5

Following the same formula guidelines, write up this next account as a news story for a local weekly newspaper. Write a *maximum of 100 words* (length is very important). Cut out the adjectives. By the way, watch it. If you haven't taken on board all I've told you about sticking to facts, you're probably going to get this wrong.

You followed an ambulance on Friday 21 December. You had only three hours to get your story to the editor before the paper went to press. Here is the information you got when you briefly interviewed Alice Jones, Michael Ford and the girls' mother.

Before you write up the story, read it through *at least twice*. Analyse it – pick out the six salient factors and write them on a Story Lead Form to give you a structure.

Then write the first paragraph. That will take approximately 50 words.

You then have 50 more words for the rest of the story. Remember, a journalist seldom uses all the information available. Decide which are the most important additional points and put them in the last 50 words.

*The people you interviewed:*

Mrs Alice Jones who lives in Talbot Street, said: 'I came in from shopping about 5 p.m. and found two little girls lying dead on the crown of the road opposite my house. They were both horribly, severely injured – blood all over them, they looked terrible, poor things. I could see they were dead. I called the ambulance, which came quickly.

'There were no cars or people in sight when I found them. Talbot Street is a quiet road with pretty woods on one side. My house is on a very sharp bend. One child wore a blue dress, the other a pink one.'

Mr Michael Ford, a teacher at Mayfield School, said: 'The children were sisters. They left the school together at about four o'clock. Jane Porter (7) was very good at drawing. Sarah (8) wasn't good at drawing at all but showed a lot of promise at cookery. They were both in Class B.

'The children lived only about ten minutes from the school and went home alone. The one hazard they had to face was crossing Talbot Street. But it's a very quiet road with hardly any traffic. Talbot Street bends sharply not far from the school and teachers are always warning children not to cross on the bend, but walk on 100 yards further where there's a zebra crossing.'

The girls' mother said (very distressed): 'We parents have appealed for two years, but nothing has been done about this road. We want the crossing moved, but you can't have a zebra on a bend. We suggested a lollipop lady on duty at the bend so children can go to her for help across the road.'

*Please, don't look at Answer 5 for my version until you've written up the story. Otherwise, you're cheating nobody but yourself. This is based on a real incident (I've changed the names, of course) and it's important for your future writing that you get this particular exercise right.*

*You can't get it wrong if you stick to the formula guidelines.*

# Chapter 6

# How to Sell Your Writing

- How to sell it
- Market research
- Reader profile

- Target readership
- The editor's problems

---

'IT's nice when writers actually *read* the magazines. So often the piece is too long, too short, or of a genre we don't run.'

PETER FIDDICK, Editor, *The Listener*

---

**W**E'RE NOW getting closer to the lovely money – selling your work. In the two previous chapters we covered news reporting. I gave you the formula for pure journalism, and you wrote two news stories. As mentioned before, there are many, many ways of writing up the same news story correctly. Much depends on which of the six factors the writer considers to be the most important, plus their individual skills and experiences.

If, after checking the answer, you got some of it wrong, don't agonise over it. Be positive and look at what you got right.

I do have one vital point to make on the 100-word story exercise. If anywhere you mentioned a car, then you didn't remember that news reporting is strictly to do with FACTS. Nowhere in the exercise was a car mentioned. Go back and check.

The post mortem revealed that the two sisters had been raped and beaten to death with a heavy object. The killer dumped their bodies on the road hoping people would think they were the victims of a hit-and-run driver.

So you, the reporter, mustn't ASSUME. Stop and think. Many things are not what they appear to be. For instance, there's that perpetuated falsehood: 'The sun comes up, and the sun goes down.'

News reporting is one of the skills that can only be learnt by DOING IT – many, many times. It's the good old trial and error method. It's up to you. You get out of this book what you put into it. Practise. Dream up situations, then write them up as news stories. Or better still, take printed stories and rewrite them to a higher standard. Look through your local papers (especially the down-market freebies) and find opening paragraphs you can shorten and improve. Be critical. Be analytical.

Your aim is always to REDUCE THE NUMBER OF WORDS. That goes whatever piece of journalism you're writing. Ask editors why they reject beginner writers and you'll find a main reason is verbal diarrhoea. Amateurs use lots of words, thinking 'the longer it is, the more I'll get paid'. But the opposite is the case. Unnecessary words are called padding, and no editor pays for them. Rather than spend the time cutting, they'll reject the piece. News reporting is a classic example of crisp, concise writing.

## How to sell it

So, now to tackling selling your writing – or MARKETING as it's known in the trade. This is in its logical order because, as you know, if you don't want rejections you must decide on the market BEFORE you start writing your feature, profile or whatever.

This book is about journalism, which is writing that's PAID FOR. It's aimed at showing you how to make money by your pen. Only the rich and foolish write for free. Like most professionals, my pen pays my mortgage. And you're not a journalist till you have a steady flow of acceptance cheques arriving in the post.

The first lesson to be learned is that a piece won't sell unless a goodly number of people want to read it. Do you think that's too basic? You'd be surprised at the number of beginners who think they merely have to write something and it'll be accepted. They're so astonished when editors reject.

Perhaps their favourite sport is squash, say, so they blithely write on how much they enjoy playing, and can't understand why it's chucked back at them. And it could have been written to a very professional standard.

But they were unrealistic. What they didn't stop to consider was, who on earth is interested in how much *they* enjoy squash? Just who are they anyway? No editor will take a piece on the joys of squash unless it is by a squash champion or perhaps a celebrity who plays.

Of course, if you're *seriously* into any sport you can write for magazines that specialise in it. But these pieces still can't be essays on 'What a lovely time I had last Thursday on the tennis court', 'Watching motor racing', or 'My side slaughtering that other mob'. You can't be subjective. Readers don't want to know how you enjoy *your* sport. They're concerned with how they can better enjoy *theirs*.

This is a bitter pill to swallow. Nobody, but NOBODY, is interested in you unless you're famous or a specialist. This also applies to your views – *unless* THEY BENEFIT THE READER IN SOME WAY. So, taking it that, like me, nobody reading this book is famous, if we want to get into print WE MUST WRITE SOMETHING THAT IS OF ADVANTAGE TO THE READER.

What could this be? Readers are always interested in something NEW, and in benefits. They'd be keen to discover how to save money when taking a holiday, buying a car, engaging a solicitor, you name it.

## A new angle

Back to squash. They could indeed be interested in a piece by Mr or Ms Nouveau-journalist IF IT HAD A GOOD ANGLE. I defined 'angle' at the end of the first chapter – a specific aspect of a subject.

A selling angle on squash could be new rules recently introduced (if there were any); new designer fashions to wear on court; a new squash complex being built. Notice – all NEWS. They're all benefits to players. So they'll pay money to buy a newspaper or magazine that carries the tips. And in turn, editors will pay the journalists for the new information.

# Market research

How do you discover what editors will accept? You make an appointment with yourself to spend at least half an hour in the largest newsagent you can find. What you're doing is Market Research. Take a notebook.

STEP ONE  Scrutinise EVERY magazine and newspaper they have. Walk slowly, get a really good look. Skim through the ones you think you'd like to write for. Make a note of their titles plus frequency (that's daily/weekly/monthly/quarterly), and price.

STEP TWO  Possibly on another day. Have another hunt. This time you're more familiar with what's on offer. Buy as many of the ones that interest you as you can afford. Get receipts as you can set these off against tax as legitimate journalistic expenses.

The publications you buy form the basis of your referral system which you'll build up over the years. Keep them in a specific box. List those you can't afford, and buy later. Also beg, borrow or steal from friends and neighbours. Ask them to save copies for you. For a thorough assessment you need AT LEAST FOUR SUCCESSIVE ISSUES of each title. This will take four weeks if it's a weekly, of course, or four months if a monthly. NB: don't forget that your public library takes many magazines and newspapers.

STEP THREE  *Study* them. First read them as a reader, subjectively, cover to cover, including the adverts. Then shift gear mentally and read right through again as a writer, *objectively*, analysing them.

What you're compiling is a list of facts about each title. Have a separate index card or computer file for each. Apart from title, frequency, cover price, address, phone and fax numbers, you need the name of the publisher, editor and – VERY IMPORTANT – the FEATURES EDITOR. That's the person journalists approach – and you always address them by name. If the name isn't printed, ring and ask for it. And, VITAL, get the spelling right.

If you consistently study the market, you'll gradually learn to recognise the DIFFERENCES between one publication from another. I cover differentiating between magazines in Chapter 19.

Bear in mind that publications don't stand still. They evolve to keep abreast of readers' demands. They also have a high staff turnover. It's very common for the editor and features editor to stay only a year or two, then move on. So, if you have a saleable idea today, and your file copies of your target magazine are a year old, go and buy a couple more to get the current position on editorial staff and contents.

# Reader profile

On your card index or computer file you're also aiming to build up a picture of the reader. It's known in the trade as a READER PROFILE. You won't be able to assess accurately what they want to read till you know their sex, level of intellect, affluence and age group, plus whether they're upmarket, midmarket or downmarket.

A very good indication is the ADVERTS. Now how do you think they help indicate the type of reader? They give an accurate indication of their INTERESTS, of what they're in the consumer goods market for. The journal's reader profile is the result of their advertising manager's market research.

If there are lots of ads for sports cars you'll know readers must be car enthusiasts. So road tests would make a subject for a SALEABLE feature. Provided – what? You say something NEW.

What else do lots of sports car ads tell you about the reader? That they are most likely male; as sports cars are two-seaters he's not a family man – therefore probably in the 20s to 30s age group, and certainly yuppie-affluent.

If the publication has ads for expensive perfume you'll know it's aimed at women who don't count pennies. It certainly isn't for the non-working wife of an office clerk or postman. That's the sort of info the ads give you.

Some publications will send you a reader profile. You might have to convince them you're going to book advertising space. Ring the Advertising Department and ask for a Media Pack.

I went into a large newsagents and asked a few customers how they choose a magazine. One 28-year-old woman was very articulate:

I sum up the contents of the magazine by the cover girl. If she's dressed very glamorously, with too much make-up and jewellery and probably looking bored, I guess that inside will be expensive adverts, clothes and shops all way beyond my income.

If she's young, freckled and wearing a mini-skirt I know the inside will be immature and gossipy.

If the cover girl has a healthy, glowing, natural look with shiny hair and little or no make-up she's the one I want to identify with – healthy not wealthy.

Another *very* useful source for readership info is *British Rate & Data*. This monthly directory lists advertising rates and circulation figures, classifying publications by subject. Look in your local reference library.

Taking a specific magazine, *Options*, you'll discover from subjects covered in the editorial and items advertised for sale, that the *Options* reader is an upmarket, educated woman who's intelligent, often a careerist, usually single so has money to spend on herself. She goes to the theatre, art galleries and big social events like Ascot and Henley.

You'd never write for this reader in the same way as for the person who takes *Woman's Weekly*. Here there'll be tips on delicious ways to prepare the cheaper cuts of meat. This is indicative of a low income. You probably won't find a recipe for lobster thermidor. There'll always be features and ads dealing with babies and children.

The *Woman's Weekly* reader is usually a mum, possibly with a part-time job as a supermarket checkout operator. You couldn't sell a feature on an obscure art gallery or barracuda fishing to *Woman's Weekly* because they are quite out of the reader's sphere of interests or means. But it's a good market for profiles on TV soap stars or someone like a woman who has fostered dozens of disabled children. They would also be in the market for features such as getting the best from a caravan holiday.

Is it now becoming clear to you why market research must logically come BEFORE you put pen to paper if you want to SELL what you write?

A trap for the would-be journalist is saying, 'Oh yes, Sarah takes *Practical Computing* or *Woman and Home* or the *Spectator* or whatever; I know what that's like.' You don't. You have read it, so you have only a subjective impression. You haven't *analysed* it.

Why do some beginner writers look upon market research as being beneath them? It's the absolute give-away that you're an amateur if you write the piece before you know your market. This is natural, of course. Writing anything at all is such a big step, beginners gets so pixilated with the mere idea of writing that they do that first. This is why they have so many rejections.

Please note this down. For experienced writers the sequence is:

(a) idea for feature/profile is born,
(b) next thought is WHERE CAN I SELL IT? Which publication has readers who want to know about it?
(c) next thought is WHAT do those readers want to know about that subject so I can tailor the piece to their demand?

## Target readership

All publications' contents and style are governed by their readers' circumstances. The main ones are gender, age, intellect, income, interests, plus market level (upmarket, midmarket or downmarket).

This also shows you what research is necessary and, therefore, which people you need to interview. Adopting this method will avoid the rejection/dejection syndrome which you'd certainly get if you sent a piece on drug pushers, say, to *Gardener's Weekly* or *Investor's Chronicle*.

Take this on board. *Very often, the only difference between people who're published and those who aren't is NOT lack of talent, but lack of marketing knowhow.*

In the last 20 to 30 years publishing has altered radically. That's because it has to keep up with readers' changing lifestyles and attitudes. Only writers who recognise this will be successful.

Gone are the days when one could write a 'cosy little piece' and have it accepted. *The Lady* doesn't expect journalism, but takes general articles, and is a traditionally 'easy market'. Even they are changing with the times. And *She* used to sparkle with pieces from new writers. It had a unique format. But it was redesigned in 1990 and now looks like all its sister magazines.

Charles Dickens, one of my heroes, was a journalist as well as a novelist. But if he was alive today and wrote his journalistic pieces as he did a century or so ago, they wouldn't be published. Why? Because the world is a different place. His work is a classic example of how the world was in the first half of the nineteenth century – and as such is revered. It is not held up as an example of writing for *today's* readers.

Cars, phones, planes, computers and space travel have speeded up the PACE of our lives. And this applies to most children and adults, including many retired people. Pensioners are not involved in the five-day-week ratrace, but quite a few of them have started a second career or are thoroughly involved with pursuing art, craft and/or academic projects. Unfortunately, few people have the TIME to read long, literary sentences. Today's writing must be crisp, less verbose.

## Understand the editor's problems

Let me show you a little of publishing through the eyes of an editor. If you know some of the problems it will help you understand some of the reasons for rejection.

It would be an ideal world if there was a simple list of rules to follow to get into print. Rules do exist. I'm giving them to you. But the ultimate intangible is the editor's gut reaction. That's what she's paid for.

Her job is to make money for the owner(s) of the publication. How does she do this? By selling thousands of copies. Magazine and newspaper publishing is a cut-throat business. Big god Profit grasps the reins in a fist of steel. The editor's skill is having her finger on the pulse of what a specific section of the reading public will BUY. This is the publication's Target Readership. The editor is constantly desperate for non-fiction that's interesting, informative and entertaining enough to make readers put their hands in their pockets.

I really mean desperate. If the publication is weekly, she has to fill 52 editions a year. Most editors rely a great deal on freelance work. BUT, of all the pieces offered her by freelances, *only five to ten per cent is written to a professional standard or is an idea her readers want and hasn't recently been used.* How do you know whether it's recently been used? You study the latest editions of the publication in the newsagent's or public library.

Think about it. If you were an editor, wouldn't you be in despair about freelance writers? Indeed, some editors have been disappointed by freelances so many times they won't consider unsolicited work. Three that come to mind are all women's magazines – *Woman's Own, Cosmopolitan* and *Company*.

OK, you say, so why's it so difficult to get work accepted? Publications *are* desperate for contributions, but not so much so that they're prepared to drop their standards.

If the editor doesn't print what the reader wants, sales will fall. And guess whose head is on the block? *That's* why they have to be so choosy.

# Chapter 7

# More on Selling

- What an editor wants
- Guidelines

- Opportunities in dailies, weeklies, monthlies, quarterlies and on radio

---

EDITOR and best-selling novelist Michael Moorcock completed ten books in one year. Does this ability stem from having been a journalist? 'Yes, learning to hit deadlines, there not being any choice, you develop the kind of discipline necessary.'

---

SOME EDITORS willingly extend a helping hand to new writers.

For instance, I was speaking to Sue Peart, editor of the *Sunday Express* colour magazine. She told me that, where freelances are concerned, what she expected first and foremost was RELIABILITY. Amateurs don't or won't appreciate that deadlines are sacrosanct – the demands of publishing dictate that come hell or high water the edition is published on deadline. Nothing, but nothing, stands in its way. (Even if the press breaks down, I've known all the plates [pages] to be flown to a printer in another country to get the issue out on time.) No, publishing doesn't acknowledge *anybody's* domestic problems, including those of the writer.

What if you wanted to write for the Sundays?

Sue Peart has always been on the look-out for new journalists with a professional approach and a genuine understanding of the importance of deadlines. Why? Because she has such a small stable of freelances whom she regularly commissions.

She was kind enough to tell me her criteria for new writers;

51

which I give you here. These guidelines are useful because, of course, they apply to many other publications, but don't expect the same treatment from all editors.

# To be studied BEFORE writing for a Sunday supplement

1  *Acquaint yourself* THOROUGHLY with the publication you intend to approach. I'm often sent lists of entirely unsuitable ideas for the *Sunday Express Magazine*. I'm forever wasting time re-directing writers to other magazines.

2  *Exclusivity:* an editor is flattered to know a prospective contributor wants to write for her/him and that they're not just on the receiving end of a round robin.

3  *Find out the* NAME of the Commissioning Editor/Features Editor. This is usually on the masthead. Or make a quick phone call to the publication's switchboard operator.

4  *Prepare a list of ideas;* SPECIALITY is no bad thing – you can tell the editor you have a particular interest in sports-royals-personality interviews etc.

5  *Grammar etc:* national publications expect perfect grammar, syntax, spelling and punctuation. It's not the editors's job to correct them.

6  *To ring or write?* It's better to WRITE in the first instance – introduce yourself and attach a list of ideas. The editor will either write back or phone. If you don't hear for a fortnight, phone her. Only ring in the first instance if you have a SCOOP that is EXACTLY RIGHT for that particular publication and can't wait for letters to be exchanged.

7  If the editor is interested in your idea, then ASK FOR A VERY EXACT BRIEF: you want to get it right and write for them again. Check on word length, angle and deadline. Let the editor know how you'll deliver the copy – by special post, fax or by bike.

8 *Don't discuss* MONEY *at this stage* as your piece may not be accepted. When you've sent in your piece and the editor rings to let you know it's fine, THEN you ask how much the fee will be, whether you should submit an invoice, and whether you can claim expenses. Rates are flexible. The experienced writer with a proven track record is paid more than the first-timer. (See my comments in Chapter 20 under 'Editors on the Phone'.)

9 *Forging a relationship with an editor*. Your first piece has been printed, both you and the editor are delighted with it. Phone and say how pleased you are and suggest meeting for a coffee or drink to discuss new ideas you have. The editor will be much more relaxed now she knows you can PRODUCE THE GOODS.

I commission a small bank of freelance writers, each with their individual approaches and interests. And I work very hard to get to know them as people so there's an understanding between us. That way, when I brief a writer, they immediately know what I want. Similarly, if they suggest an idea, I can immediately say 'yes' or 'no' because I know exactly what I'm going to get.

10 *Read the papers to keep abreast of the* NEWS. At any time an editor might ring out of the blue wanting a piece written quickly about some recent event. She will expect you to know about it. If you don't, she'll expect you to find out through cuttings.

I have occasionally been exasperated explaining a news story to a writer who responds with: 'Oh, I *never* read the tabloids' *or* 'I *never* watch TV'. It would have been quicker and more effective to have written the piece myself.

11 RELIABILITY – If you can't do a piece, say so! Occasionally a feature needs to be turned in very fast. It's no admission of failure to refuse because you're going on holiday/got a children's tea party/six other deadlines.

12 *Don't play off one magazine against another*. The colour supplement market is a very tight network and editors know what the others are up to. Forge a relationship with one and

stay loyal. By all means write for other newspapers or magazines, providing they're not rivals.

# Frequencies

Let's look at acceptance opportunities by various publication
categories. First, frequency. This is one of the ways you can get
good mileage from a single newsy idea. Publications of different
frequencies aren't usually rivals. So, you can safely write up your
idea from four different angles. Submit one to a daily, another to a
weekly, the third to a monthly and the last to a quarterly.

In addition, you can often submit yet another version to radio.

# Dailies

The journals that take the largest number of short, non-fiction
pieces from freelances are the national Press. Why? Coming out
daily, they have more than 300 editions a year and that's a lot of
space to fill. They are among the highest payers and are the
ultimate goal of a good many professional journalists.

As long as your work is up to their standard there's no reason
why beginners can't make the national dailies and Sundays. A
good number of my students do. But topicality is usually a beginner's stumbling block. Topicality is the god of newspapers. Journalists have to write their news features FAST – often in a matter of
hours from pen to editor's desk. Few neophyte writers can work at
that speed and be accurate. You've got to hit the ground running –
and keep going. But it does develop after long practise.

However, other types of features popular with the national
Press, and less pressurised, are pieces on CURRENT SOCIAL ISSUES.
The topic could be litter on the streets, the plight of carers for
mentally handicapped or aged relatives, the increasing amount of
drug-related crime. Many freelances specialise in writing up-to-
date pieces on those types of issues. The angle is that it's the
LATEST DEVELOPMENTS. See? news again.

# Weeklies

The next largest market for freelances – local Press, magazines of daily and Sunday nationals, and what are known as newsmagazines. They're magazine format but contain plenty of newsy pieces, they're all concerned with what's happening NOW. What's in the news? Some newsmag titles are *News Week*, *New Statesman*, *Economist*, *Melody Maker*, *NME*, *Time Out*, *City Limits*, *Chat*, *Best*, *Bella* and *Me*, and, in London, freebies like *Midweek*, *Girl About Town*, *Ms London* and *Nine to Five*. Every big city has its free job vacancy newsmagazines.

Topicality is also of mega-importance to them. They want immediacy, not history. They have to fill 52 editions a year and accept a LOT of freelance material. Their rates of pay vary, but some are very attractive. Most beginners are capable of writing for their local paper and the newsmagazines.

Another section of weeklies are what are known as specialist publications such as *Nursing Times*, *Money Week* and *Match* – there's a great variety. There's also the very lucrative female market – for example *Woman's Weekly*, *My Weekly*, *Woman*, *Woman's Own* and *Woman's Realm*. These aren't newsmags and lack the impact of that genre, so if speed scares you, they're your market. They like up-to-date gossip on people like Joan Collins and Princess Di. (NB. Some of them don't take unsolicited material – check.)

# Monthlies

Coming out only 12 times a year, monthlies offer freelance journalists fewer opportunities. But their plus side is that they take more in-depth pieces. They also have a greater number of pages and a far longer lead time. (More jargon. 'Lead time' is the amount of time you have to prepare your work before their press date.)

But even monthlies plan a long way ahead – usually four to six months. Be aware, for instance, that if you want to submit a piece about Christmas, then August is too late.

The reason magazines have to work so far ahead is partly editorial and partly advertising. Each edition is planned in detail. At the time of the first editorial meeting the entire content won't be ready to hand. For balance, a number of pieces have still to be written. They'll be commissioned either from staffers or regular freelances and those writers have to be given a decent length of time to research and interview.

Additionally, the advertising department needs a period of time to sell enough space to make sure the magazine's bank account isn't in the red after publication.

What all this means to the general freelance is usually what seems like a ridiculous deadline. Possibly it will be four to six months before publication date. This is exacerbated by the fact that most monthlies appear in the newsagents at least two weeks before the month printed on their cover. But it's up to you to ensure your piece on Easter reaches the editor in September, and a feature on Hallowe'en will be wanted in April.

You'll need to be just as bright-eyed and bushy-tailed about long lead times if you write for specialist magazines. If your particular speciality is sport, say, from the date of your Big Annual Event you need to count back four to five months for your deadline. For the Boat Race, submit the previous October, for the Derby, the previous January. If you don't, another journalist will.

The monthlies are mostly specialist titles on sport, leisure interests, careers and commerce, plus a large proportion of women's upmarket titles – and ALL the men's titles like *Playboy* and *GQ*.

# Quarterlies

Quarterlies are thin on the ground, but they include a series very popular with new writers – the COUNTIES. As you may know, dozens of counties have their own glossy, full colour publications, eg *Dorset Life*, *Warwickshire World*, and *Lincolnshire Life*. They take 'general articles', so their standard isn't particularly high. They're an ideal jumping-off place. But they have two distinct disadvantages:

1   If accepted, it'll be probably at least a year before you see your work in print and get paid for it. Most publications, whatever their frequency, pay on appearance, not acceptance.

2 Experienced journalists don't usually touch the counties because these magazines don't carry much clout with the more 'commercial' editors when they ask for clips of an author's printed work to discover the standard of their writing.

When a person a publication has never heard of suggests an idea for a piece, if the editor likes it, he'll say: 'Yes, I could be interested, but I need to see what you've done first. Send me cuttings of recent work you've had published.' If you send clips of things you've had accepted by any of the county magazines, or publications like *The Lady* perhaps, they won't carry a great deal of weight; although those are certainly better than sending things you've had in parish magazines or duplicated 'arty' newsletters, or fanzines (magazines brought out by fans about their favourite rock star or hobby).

# Radio

In addition to print, remember many a good idea can be used for radio – yet more mileage for that single idea. So think up an angle suitable for one of the programmes. I cover radio in Chapter 23.

# Chapter 8

# Yet More on Selling

- Approaching editors
- Outlines
- Your credentials
- Exercise 6

- Research
- Check your facts
- Newspaper Library
- Finding time to write

---

'ONE writer sent a query letter misspelling both the company name and mine. Another way to lose an assignment is by not catching my attention in the first two lines.'

ED RABINOWITZ, Editor, *Volkswagen's World* (USA)

---

LACKING the confidence to send work to a publication is natural. You're not alone in this particular pool of terror. We've all swum in it. Faith in yourself must be the motivation: 'I've applied all I've learned about journalism, I've done my best, I KNOW it's a good idea.'

The fact that editors are more likely to accept work from proven writers is tough. But look at this analogy.

Let's say your livelihood, your survival, depends on your job as a factory manager. Your company has a reputation for making quality shoes. Lots of others try to emulate you, so you have to keep an eye on quality to maintain your reputation and sales.

You have always bought your leather from a tanner who supplies only top-grade skins.

You're offered cheaper leather by a tanner you've never heard of before. You only have his word that his skins are excellent.

Which supplier do you buy from?

Buying from the newcomer is a commercial and economic risk. But if the newcomer can point to another manufacturer he's supplied whose shoes have satisfied customers, you'd be more likely to risk buying his skins, wouldn't you?

By the same logic, an editor prefers to buy work from writers with a proven track record.

Collect as many by-lines as you can. They're your debenture, your only legitimate way of proving your track record.

## Approaching editors

So, you have your brilliant idea for a news feature, profile or review. You've been to your newsagent and had a good look at all those dozens of publications. You've picked out a few that publish pieces on similar subjects. And they haven't recently used an angle remotely resembling yours. Right. The next step is to SELL it.

There's very little point in going to all the trouble of writing it if you're not going to be able to sell it. Few professionals write on spec. They make sure they're going to be accepted BEFORE they start writing.

It's the least frustrating and time-wasting method both for the editor and you. EDITORS WOULD FAR RATHER BE APPROACHED BEFOREHAND so that they can say whether or not the idea interests them, and if so, how they want it written up. They're only too pleased to tell you. And this applies universally, from newspapers right through to the glossy monthlies.

## An outline is your ambassador

The best method is to send in an OUTLINE.

You can phone with the idea first if you like. But if the editor's interested, he'll often still ask for a written outline of anything that's 500 words and more, rather than the finished work.

Anyway, editors can be a bit daunting to phone. As I've said before, they work at a furious pace, always in production meetings. They don't take kindly to amateurs ringing them. Indeed, their secretaries are trained to be a buffer between them and the outside world.

# What an outline does

An outline *briefly* explains the IDEA, ie the SUBJECT plus the new ANGLE you have on it.

Take as much TIME over the outline as over the actual feature. It's your salesman. It will sell the piece before it's written. You might even get a commission.

Another point. It often makes a big difference to the piece in that you'll suggest angle 'A', and the editor could write back saying yes, and will you also include 'X'. Or he might even suggest angle 'B' instead of 'A'. It might well be an interesting aspect that hadn't occurred to you. It would certainly be a relevant one, as the editor has a finger on the pulse of what readers want.

# What exactly is an outline

It is more than a summary. It must accentuate what's NEW and DIFFERENT about YOUR viewpoint.

The letter must give shape to the idea so that the editor can see it on the page. It must exude ENTHUSIASM because, being such a good idea, readers will be dying to read it. It should also convey confidence – not to be confused with arrogance, which would probably result in a straight refusal.

# How to start

Begin the outline with the SUBJECT PLUS ANGLE – in the FIRST PAR.

Why? An editor who has to wade through lots of words before discovering what the proposal is about, is an irritated editor. That's the wrong frame of mind for you to create if you're after acceptance. Anyway, a lengthy outline indicates a verbose, amateur writer, and you've lost before you start.

The MAXIMUM LENGTH IS ONE SIDE OF AN A4 PAGE. If an editor has to turn to yet another page just to discover the extent of your idea he finds it a real put-off.

Don't send a letter *and* an outline, they're all one. Don't waffle. Think out exactly what you want to say before writing. Make several drafts first.

For heaven's sake *don't* start: 'I am a journalist. I am writing to ask . . .' It's so crass. Some editors wouldn't read any further. If you were writing to a greengrocer's to sell them 50 boxes of apples you wouldn't start: 'I am a fruitgrower . . .' And why *state* I am writing'? – he can *see* your words on the page, he doesn't need you to tell him.

Start straight in along the lines: 'Would you be interested in 1000 words on the effects of X on Z?'

State as briefly as possible how you would develop the idea. 'Banning cars from the centre of the city can be achieved by XX. The advantages are (a), (b), and (c). Disadvantages are so-and-so.'

It's important to give the editor confidence in your profession-alism by following that with POSITIVE sentences like 'I will argue both sides of . . .', 'I will supply photos of . . .', 'I will reveal . . .', 'I will interview Mr . . .'. But these mustn't be merely carrots to tempt the editor – no more than good intentions on your part.

Beware of making promises you can't keep. Think out beforehand the amount of research necessary and whether you can cope. Ensure BEFORE you write that you *can* deliver the goods. Otherwise you'll be very embarrassed later. Not only that, if you promise, say, quotes from a consultant cardiologist and don't produce them, you'll very likely be rejected. And you'll ruin your chances of building up goodwill with that editor for future acceptances.

State the relevant factors you'll use in your piece like statistics, quotations, anecdotes, topical interest, celebrity views.

Start with the specific and work towards the general – ALWAYS History and exposition, if used, come last.

## Specialisation helps

If you have some credible, relevant experience of the subject, then say so: 'As a qualified nurse, I will explore the effects of coping with a relative's grief when a patient dies', or 'I regularly play the piano in a club. I will discuss stress experienced by musicians working till 3 a.m. night after night.'

# Your credentials

As you're unknown the editor will need some sort of proof that you can write. He'll ask you for cuttings of your published work, with your by-line on them, hopefully. Send photocopies, never originals, as they're seldom returned.

If you haven't any to offer yet, just keep quiet and pray you won't be asked. Just the occasional editor might forget. And what else do you always enclose? A STAMPED ADDRESSED ENVELOPE.

A GOOD OUTLINE SELLS THE PIECE IN ADVANCE. That's what marketing is all about.

## EXERCISE 6

Write an outline of the angle you thought up for *Exercise 2* to sell it to the editor of the publication you chose. Now you're further along in this book and have done your market research, you might want to change your mind about that first angle you thought up. You might have come up with a better one, or a different publication for which you would prefer to write.

The outline letter mustn't be more than one side of an A4 page long; the shorter the better, actually. Write it before you look at *Answer 6*, the example I've written for you.

# Research

A professional journalist can write 1,000 words on any subject.

Conversely, few journalists need to know very much about anything. What they DO KNOW is WHERE TO FIND OUT. Journalists become expert researchers, investigators.

Citing my own experiences – I remember writing 5,000 words for the architectural press on the merits of various types of alloy cladding on commercial buildings. I couldn't even attempt to discuss the subject now; at the time I became an instant expert because it was necessary for the feature.

I've also written on electronic safety devices for construction engineers on oil rigs and the pharmacokinetics of certain drugs in the bodies of people with Parkinson's disease. All heavy subjects.

The only way I became knowledgeable enough to write plausible features was through research.

# Check your facts

And you've got to get your facts correct. It's Murphy's Law that if you don't, some beastly 12-year-old swot will write to your editor and put him right. Editors don't like that. Result: he's lost confidence in you for ever. Editors don't forget brickbats from readers.

Research can be a mega project. It's a skill in its own right. People earn their living as researchers. If you're up against a tight deadline you can engage them to do it for you (for a hefty fee, of course). Look for researchers in the *Writers' & Artists' Yearbook*.

So, you're writing a feature. You've thought of a good angle. What you now need is solid background info to give the piece substance. Where do you find it? What's step number one?

Your own cuttings files, notebooks and reference books. There's a lot to be said for investing in a reputable, secondhand encyclopaedia. Those of us with adapted TV sets can access Ceefax or Oracle.

What's step number two? The public reference library. In addition to books they'll have several editions of national and regional newspapers plus a computerised bonanza of info they can access at speed. This should include invaluables like the Humanities Index which lists features published on thousands of subjects, starting with abortion.

# National Newspaper Library

The journalist's indispensable National Newspaper Library is at Hendon, opposite Colindale underground station on the Northern Line. They have copies of most newspapers and magazines from launch to now.

Well, almost all. In 1940 a German bomber wiped out a million Irish and provincial newspapers in 10,000 bound volumes. Thankfully they were only a fraction of the library's acquisition. There are now 20 miles of shelving to support their gargantuan collection of 650,000 volumes.

There's a reading room (all seats permanently occupied, it seems!) Make an appointment to visit (tel: 071-636 1544). What's nice is that you tell them what you want to see, and when you arrive the newspapers or magazines are waiting for you.

If you're writing about products or services, another tip is to contact the supplier's Public Relations department. The leaflets they send you will be invaluable. Their press releases will possibly be abysmally written, but with persistence you will be able to dig out the genuine information. (NB: too many press releases are blatant self-congratulation and eulogisation couched in moronic English. That's why I said PR is full of failed journalists.)

The *Daily Telegraph* used to be ultra-efficient at researching 'difficult' queries for you. I've never been failed by them. But in 1990 they stopped doing research and the service was taken on by an independent company (tel: 071–924 4414).

The first step in all research is to FIND OUT WHERE TO FIND OUT.

I can recommend the definitive book on the subject: *Research for Writers* by Ann Hoffmann. The author takes your hand and tells you how to start your research, the simplest and most accurate methods to use. She leads you through mazes of indexes, directories, bibliographies, guides and manuals of both British and foreign data. Public records and private papers are there, as are broadcast and TV material, special libraries and a number of unpublished sources.

# Finding time to write

Oh, the mortification – 'I *meant* to write that piece, but . . .' It really is difficult if you're not used to working alone and haven't developed the self-discipline.

Because their work is creative, writers prefer to operate solo so they can better focus their minds. So, to get down to the exercises in this book or ANY writing, actually MAKE APPOINTMENTS WITH YOURSELF. Enter 'writing time' in your diary exactly the same as for appointments with your dentist/hairdresser/tennis partner. Enter a daily appointment of two hours or more for the next three months.

What you're aiming to do is make daily writing an automatic

habit like cleaning your teeth. Dare I give you that well proven old saw 'practise makes perfect'? Journalism won't just happen, you've got to keep on doing it.

If you can't or won't make yourself write daily, then put away your pen and go and be a greengrocer. You're proving you just haven't got what it takes to be a journalist.

Don't trot out: 'I've got the kids to get off to school, go to work, look after my invalid father, keep the garden in shape, have some sort of social life'. Professionals have the same hurdles to cope with – they didn't get successful by hiding behind excuses. They got up at 5.30 a.m., seven days a week, and wrote.

# Chapter 9

# Writing Techniques

- Angle again
- Some pointers on style, including quotes, clichés and grammar
- Exercise 7
- Tuition

> 'I PLAN to write 800 words a day. If I'm falling behind, I work longer hours; and always strive to complete ahead of deadline.'
>
> GORDON WELLS, Author, *The Successful Author's Handbook*

HERE ARE some answers to those nitty gritty questions: How do the professionals do it? What makes a piece of non-fiction into a journalistic feature instead of a general article? In other words, how do you give a piece 'punch', 'verve' and 'bite'?

Did you write to an imaginary editor an outline suggesting an angle for a feature BEFORE you looked at my example? I hope you did, otherwise I'm not helping you.

Let's look at that angle you thought up for Exercise 2 (or another angle, if you prefer). You've got a publication in mind. You've even got as far as sending an outline (*Exercise 6*). PANIC STATIONS. The editor wrote back saying *Yes, she'd like to see the piece*. Heck, you're actually in business.

What's the most effective way to go about writing it up? Now I don't know what idea you've created or for what market, but that doesn't matter for the moment. The following tips apply to ALL journalistic writing, at whatever market it's targeted.

66

# Angle

Before you start, seriously ask yourself: is the piece worth writing at all? Is the ANGLE I thought up *really* unusual? Additionally, do I have the most UP-TO-DATE details about it so it tells the reader something NEW, something they didn't know before?

NEW is the basis of 'news'. NEW is the genesis of journalism. Think about the word. Jour is French for 'day', journal means 'comments on today' – daily news. It's all about NOW, all immediate, never history. If you haven't anything fresh to say then your readers aren't interested. So really think it through. Find the most interesting, up-to-date angle. Use CIPP to explore all the possibilities.

# Style

A promise from me, hand on heart – your own personal style WILL DEVELOP, naturally. And if it's firmly based on journalistic rules, it'll be a style that sells.

**DON'T OVERWRITE** Journalism for today's readership is crisp and concise. One of the biggest faults of amateurs is overwriting. Old-fashioned phrases and long sentences containing multi-syllabic words won't get accepted. Neither will the sort of prose used in office memos, academic theses or essays.

**SHORT WORDS** Use short words. In our rich and varied English language there are nearly always two or three words with closely similar meanings. Choose the shortest one.

**Examples:** obtained/got, employ/hire, deceased/dead, examine/probe, reservation/booking, be aware of/know, go and see/visit, be on the look-out/watch.

Invest in a copy of *Roget's Thesaurus*.

**SHORT SENTENCES** Vary the lengths of your sentences for interest and 'texture'. And don't let them ramble. I've already mentioned that sentences shouldn't be longer than 25 to 27 words.

**SHORT PARAS**   Paragraphs should also be short. The ideal length is no more than two or three sentences. There should also be many of them – a fresh one for each idea.

**QUOTES**   Something that always 'lifts' a piece is quotes. Can you define this? (Something someone other than the author has said.) They're known in the trade as quotes because the words are always between inverted commas, also known as quote marks.

What I *don't* mean is a quotation from a literary figure such as Shakespeare.

Quotes are also one of the three essentials that defines a short piece of non-fiction as journalism, as opposed to a 'general article' (see Chapter 2 to remind yourself of my definition of journalism and the other two vital ingredients).

Peter Gillman, who was 15 years on the *Sunday Times*, says:

> There are people who write articles indoors and there are journalists who go out to look for their stories. Journalism is not merely writing from your own experience or research in cuttings and books. It's going out and asking people questions. You need to know what you want to know. Once you've obtained your information, you can give your piece greater drive and impact by letting people speak for themselves. Quote them directly, especially when they are describing their feelings and judgements. This gives your writing immediacy and authority.

Quotes give human interest. Remember, the most successful features are about PEOPLE – this is one of the reasons for the insatiable popularity of profiles.

Interview people to get their views and quote those in your work between inverted commas.

**Example:** You're doing a piece on the Channel Tunnel. Get statements from people who think it's a great idea and expound the advantages. Get more from others who disagree, with all the disadvantages they see; this gives a balanced overview.

**Example:** You're doing a news feature on a disused church hall being turned into a community centre. Interview the person who thought up the idea; ask them, 'How did it occur to you?' And the person who raised money to fund it, 'How did you do it?' And the person on the committee that runs it, 'What events do you organise? What are future plans?' And as many people who visit it as possible, 'Do you enjoy it here? Why?' or 'Why not?'

**Example:** If you can get quotes from famous people it might be just that which sells your piece. Like it or not, big names are ultra-popular with readers. Even if you're writing on a bland subject such as garden sheds, it's probably guaranteed to be accepted if you got quotes from Jeffrey Archer on how he built his, or from Judi Dench on why she doesn't have one.

**OPINIONS**    Difficult to swallow, this, but readers aren't really interested in the opinions of beginner journalists (see letter from Jean Silvan Evans in Chapter 4). People only want to read the opinions of specialists, celebrities and journalists who have made themselves well established in print by the high quality of their work – for instance, someone such as Bernard Levin.

**VERBS FOR ACTION**    Verbs are the words that make prose ACTIVE and bring it alive. They're a journalist's most powerful words. Adjectives you use, yes, but they're more the ammunition of fiction writers.

Journalists make everything they write as lively and interesting as they can. They never use a 'gentle' verb if they can find a brisker one.

**Example:** 'Police removed the barrier' has nothing like the impact of 'Police tore down the barrier'.

**WORDS MUST WORK**    Use the least number of words possible – EVERY WORD MUST BE NECESSARY. It must have a job to do or it shouldn't be there.

**Example:** 'Despite the fact that the engine had broken down, he had manoeuvred the sailing boat with a deft skill across the stretch of water and finally into the harbour, where he secured it to a mooring.' Compare with: 'Despite engine failure, he had deftly sailed the boat into the harbour.' The second sentence is less than a third of the length of the first, but gives no less information. ('Secured it to the mooring' is unnecessary. There's only one reason an engine-less boat is taken into harbour.)

## DON'T BE OBSCURE
**Example:** This sentence doesn't 'say' anything: 'Her advice made a difference to my life'. This doesn't give the reader any information. *What* difference? Did the writer mean her life was better or worse? The use of words doesn't tell you.

**AVOID REPETITION**   In journalism you are writing for readers in a hurry.

**Example:** 'The fireman's hose doused the flames and put out the fire.' Either 'doused the flames' or 'put out the fire' is super-fluous.

**Example:** 'The brakes failed. The lorry driver kept his finger on the horn to let people know he was coming and warn them to get out of the way.' Either 'to let people know he was coming' or 'and warn them to get out of the way' is superfluous.

**ADJECTIVES ARE OFTEN UNNECESSARY**   Read Heming-way – he hated adjectives.

**Example:** All the words in italics in the following sentence are adjectives and can be easily dispensed with: 'The *strong* gale demolished the *stout* oak tree in *the short space of* three minutes.' Everyone knows a gale is a strong wind. Oaks are always stout. Nobody needs telling that three minutes isn't very long, we can all count. Re-read the sentence without the adjectives – it has much more 'bite'.

**BE POSITIVE**   Use positive words and phrases, not negative ones.

**Example:** 'The cup is half empty' is negative, 'The cup is half full' is positive.

**SAY WHAT YOU MEAN** If you don't re-read your sentences, you could confuse or seriously mislead your reader.

**Example:** 'General Eisenhower flies back to front'. This classic World War II boob headline actually appeared in print. It should have read 'General Eisenhower returns to front line', of course.

**Example:** 'He told him not to sell the shares'
'He told him now to sell the shares'
One is the complete opposite of the other. On a typewriter keyboard the 't' and 'w' aren't too far away from each other. This typo (typographical error) can easily be made.

**Example:** 'Brown got Jones put in jail because he wanted revenge.' Who wanted revenge? Brown or Jones? The sentence should be 'Brown wanted revenge, so got Jones put in jail.' Or 'Brown stopped Jones taking revenge by getting him put in jail.'

**Example:** 'He made ball bearings for juggernaut lorries which he kept in matchboxes.' I don't think you can get a juggernaut into a matchbox.

**BE ACTIVE** Write actively, not passively. I'll give you an example of that.

## EXERCISE 7

Please write down 'The man was bitten by the dog'. That's passive. Now write the exact same sentence stated actively. Write it down now before you look at *Answer 7* at the back of the book . . . OK – now look it up.

Can you see the difference? It's crisper, punchier, it's also two words shorter. Editors don't pay for padding; rather than rewrite an overwritten piece, which could take hours, they'll merely chuck it back at you.

# More on Style

**CLICHÉS** Modern journalism should be free of clichés – that's ANY often-used phrase. The rule is 'if you've heard it before, it's a cliché'.

They are certainly apt, that's why they're so often seen or heard.

But if you use them it sabotages the development of your personal style. They're somebody else's invention – somebody else's words. Lazy people always choose the easy option. Lazy writers grab the nearest cliché.

This is where you lean heavily on your creativity. Create phrases of our own which, hopefully, will be tomorrow's clichés because you have been so inventive.

The only instances where clichés are legitimately allowed are:

(a)  in quotes when someone else uses them, but don't overdo them or the person you're quoting will sound crass, or
(b)  when used deliberately as a sort of pun, a play on words.

**Examples:** 'Man's inhumanity to woman' and 'Let's look at the fax of life' (title of a survey on facsimile machines); and the title of a road safety feature, 'Children should be seen and not hurt'. Clichés used this way can be very powerful.

Otherwise, clichés are the mark of an amateur writer or a politician. Do you, as a journalist, want the same reputation as that of an MP? In speeches in the House they too often trade clichés instead of ideas. The aim of many MPs is to talk a great deal but SAY NOTHING. Journalists must be braver than politicians. Journalists must be honest.

Your best friend here is *Roget's Thesaurus*.

Incidentally, do you do crossword puzzles? They're great for synonyms and for improving spelling.

**SPLIT INFINITIVES**   If you're not careful you can confuse your reader by splitting infinitives. Can you define one?

**Example:** 'To boldly go'. It should be 'to go boldly'. The verb is 'to go' and those two words belong together. They shouldn't be split by other words.

**Example:** (I read this on a government instruction sheet) 'Fill the green, A4 size, application form in'. Which is the verb there? – 'fill in', of course.

Yes, infinitives are split all the time. English is a delightfully colloquial language. And they're acceptable unless the 'split' consists of such a large number of words, the reader loses sight of the first part of the verb and has to re-read to get the sense. Try not to split verbs asunder.

**GRAMMAR, SPELLING, PUNCTUATION** These are important. They're the tools of GOOD COMMUNICATION. As you know, the reason all three evolved is to make speech and writing as easy to understand as possible. THEY'RE NOT OPTIONAL EXTRAS.

Syntax and punctuation aren't the whims of some obscure academic. They ensure that what you are specifically trying to put over is understood by people who can't see inside your head and have only marks on paper in front of them.

The fact that many junior schools chucked grammar books out of the window is a serious stumbling block for anyone intending to become a wordsmith.

I was talking to the Director of the National Council for the Training of Journalists. He lamented the dismally poor standard of English of people trying to get into the profession.

He said the industry is in despair, with so many sub-standard people applying for jobs. Often the only reason they don't get taken on is because they fail tests in the Queen's English. They don't know a comma from a semi-colon – don't understand possessive commas – can't distinguish 'was' from 'were', or affect from effect – don't understand tenses – can't conjugate verbs – can't spell. This even applies to English graduates.

Too often people want the fast lane glamour of journalism but aren't prepared to learn the basics. Neither do they show responsibility towards maintaining standards of the English language.

The Director mainly blamed the sloppy way today's teens and twenties were taught at school. But, if they want to become wordsmiths, just as with any trade or profession, they've got to have a sound knowledge of the fundamentals. In this case, grammar, syntax, punctuation and spelling.

Jobs are going to older people who cut their milk teeth on the rigorous rules of the three Rs.

I'm not personally berating you here, but passing on what the Director told me. *You* know if you're at all shaky on English. If you are I recommend a superb book, Fowler's *Modern English Usage*. It's long been the definitive work explaining all the ins and outs. And there's an invaluable pocket-size volume similar to Fowler's called *The Oxford Miniguide to English Usage*. Another helpful volume is *Essential Grammar in Use* by Raymond Murphy. And there are many others. Get yourself to a really large bookshop and see what's on offer. Discover which book deals best with your particular problem.

For spelling, get the best authoritative dictionary you can afford, Oxford, Chambers, Collins etc. Get a large one which gives adverbs and other endings.

# Tuition

Of course, the best method is having a tutor take you through basic grammar. To any student who asks my advice on this I suggest an Adult Education class in *English as a Foreign Language*.

OK, so it's embarrassing to ask for help now you're an adult. but you wouldn't be among children, you'd be among people who have the same problems as yourself. If you have a frank word with the tutor, she will very likely be able to help you focus on your particular problems.

Part of being in the writing profession is to maintain the standard of the English language. I'm not being highfalutin'. A prime function of mine is to be a COMMUNICATOR. Effective communicators are wedded to the concept of making comprehension as simple as possible.

Slovenly writing is indicative of a slovenly thinker, so the author's professional approach would be in question. If he's too lazy to learn his basic craft, too lazy to look in a dictionary or English grammar book, what other facts hasn't he checked? It immediately stamps him as an amateur.

# Chapter 10

# The Real Thing

- First draft
- Structure
- Intros with impact
- Effective endings
- Exercise 8
- Writing to length
- Presentation
- Checkpoints

'WE want MSS that have been laboured over – tight writing, good sentence structure, as well as lively descriptive style that really involves the reader.'

MARGORIE H. RICE, Editor, *Bridal Fair* (USA)

THIS IS the green light. You've a great idea. Your enthusiasm is surging through your veins and creative energy is roaring down your fingers!

## First draft

Your very first stab at writing a piece since you started this book. My best advice at this stage is CRASH AWAY ON YOUR TYPEWRITER AND GET THE THING DOWN.

Don't worry if part of it is in note form, or it's littered with half-formed ideas, or clichés, or bits you suspect you'll jettison later, or if it's too long. That's what first drafts are for. What's vital is geting down on paper the general flow *while the thing is still fresh in your mind*. Spontaneity is what makes writing individual.

You will know about the right and left sides of the brain. The area we use when we're galloping through the first draft is the creative, the right side. Later we use the left, the side of logic, to put everything into good order.

Some journalists polish as they go, but the vast majority do that in later drafts, at the editing stage. Plenty of writers need three or more drafts before they get it the way they think the editor wants it to be.

There's no 'correct' number of drafts. As you're in a BUYER'S MARKET, do as many as it takes.

# Structure

Before you start creating your work, it's a great help if you make yourself some guidelines. These act as a map, which is useful on any journey. It is just a list of a few key words.

Take the Story Lead Form I showed you how to compile, even if you're using a word processor. At the top, first note three things in block caps:

(1)  the title of the publication you're writing for;
(2)  the number of words they've specified;
(3)  a brief Reader Profile (possibly something like '20-to-40-year-old upmarket women').

Those are the most vital factors. They are there as a constant reminder while you're writing.

Now your structure. You're making this map so you don't waste time digressing. You've done your research and interviewed people. You have all your information in your notebook, but jotted down in random bursts without any prior knowledge of the order in which they'll be needed.

Still on your Story Lead Form, list the major points of your piece in one or two words. Put them in logical order, so that one leads out of the other. That will give the piece a credible 'flow'. Don't dart about erratically or the work will be ragged and incomprehensible.

A list could be something along the lines of : (a) State Problem; (b) Cure it this Way; (c) Hazards to Avoid; (d) What you Achieve.

At this stage formulate your beginning AND end. Then you won't reach the final paragraph to discover you have saved nothing significant with which to round off.

Next, tackle the actual writing. Deal with the first point on your list, then go on to the next, and so on. As you write, keep glancing at the list to guide you. You'll find it a great help when you've covered such-and-such a point; you don't then say: 'Hell, what should follow this?' It's all been worked out, so you can now focus entirely on the actual writing.

Every paragraph should lead out of the previous one. Draw a parallel here between journalism and fiction. In both cases the aim is to tell a story. You not only inform, you also entertain.

These guidelines are also useful should you not be able to complete the piece at one sitting. It re-focuses the mind when you return.

# Intros must have impact

The beginning is the most important part of your feature from a selling viewpoint – and that's the one you have to aim at. That first sentence MUST grab the reader's attention. Why? To make them want to read on.

Readers are terribly transitory. All editors know this. It's even been monitored. Scientific surveys reveal that a great many of the reading public usually make hurried visits to newsagents because they have a train to catch, or want something to read on the way to work or in the coffee break. A magazine cover catches their eye; they skim through the pages scanning the text; they read only the first sentence of each piece. If it makes an impression they decide they want to read it. They buy the publication.

If nothing catches their eye, they put it down and pick up something else or leave the shop. A sale is lost.

That's why journalism doesn't work up to the high point buried later in the piece. It must be there, up at the front, in the very first sentence.

Editors cater for readers in a hurry.

## Examples of intros with impact

'Child abuse doesn't only happen in Cleveland. Not enough boroughs are tackling this we-don't-talk-about-it problem.'

Or one on a completely different subject: 'There's usually a chimpanzee at Peter's breakfast table – sometimes more than one. He's the vet for Bloggstown Zoom.'

This one opens with a quote: 'I somehow knew he was dead when I saw him lying on the pavement. And three yobbos were running away hell for leather – but too fast for me.' This was the start of a feature on victim support groups. Catapult the reader into the action in the first sentence.

Questions make good intros: 'Why are people in wheelchairs banned from most adult eduction?' (They're not of course, but the feature goes on to say that front steps and the absence of working lifts in many schools has that effect.)

Or: 'Can you fly without a plane? Members of Whitechester's new para-gliding club can.' Or even a double question opening: 'How many cancer-free years are left to people on this planet? How large will the hole in the ozone layer be in the year 2000?'

Try to answer all the questions or, at least, thrash out the arguments. Give pro and con views from interviews with a number of people and present one or more solutions.

Don't labour over the intro or delay starting because you can't think of one. It will often jump out at you from the body of the piece after you've written the first draft.

Start with the high spot, the point of your argument, the result of your research. In the next exercise, where you write the first part of a feature, I want you to concentrate on an opening with impact.

## Effective endings

When you reach the end don't just stop because you have run out of things to say. The piece must have a positive 'kicker'. It must be rounded off.

An effective way to finish off is to refer to future plans, or a solution. Assure the reader that because of action taken the problem won't occur again. Or explain all the benefits you have now you've knitted yourself a garage!

An effective way to finish off is to return to the same theme that opened the piece, but with a twist.

**Example:** This feature is about the opening of a new garden for disabled people to visit. It starts: 'Since I was in a car accident I've had to live in a wheelchair. It scuppered gardening for me. It was my biggest love.' Then follows: 'Bryan was one of the first visitors to Hanley Street Special Garden' and a description of what it looks like and how it was sponsored. It ends with another quote from Bryan: 'Visiting the new garden set me thinking. In my own plot I've now had raised flower beds built that can be worked on from a wheelchair.'

Those last two sentences could easily have gone into the main body of the feature – but a good journalist always saves something significant for the end.

Endings should always try to be positive, even if the subject is depressing. For instance, a piece on cot deaths could finish with new training courses on the subject for hospital nurses, or something like that which will reduce or help cure the problem.

## EXERCISE 8

Remember the angle you thought up for *Exercise 2?* Write up the first 100 words giving the piece an intro with real impact. Start with something dramatic if you can, or at least, something written in an attention-getting style.

Then re-write it at least twice – with a different intro each time. Finally, compare your intros and keep the best. You'll be writing the full-length piece for the next exercise.

# Why length is important

'Writing to length' means providing the exact number of words the publication's asked for.

Why do editors specify a number? It's never just a figure off the top of their heads. Every edition of every publication has to be carefully planned. The size of page determines the amount of text it can contain.

Looking at your typical magazine, the format of each month's edition is similar in that it carries a specific amount of advertising and a specific amount of editorial. The ideal profit-making ratio is 60 per cent advertising to 40 per cent editorial.

In the magazine in our example there's always, say, a short story, a longish main feature, a shorter one, a profile plus three fillers.

Taking into account that there always needs to be space for headlines or titles, the maximum number of words that the page will accommodate is 1,000 plus an illustration, or 1,250 without an illustration.

This is the regular pattern. Two pages are apportioned for the short story – as it is never illustrated it's always 2,500 words. Another two pages are always allocated to the main feature, so that can't be over 2,250 words as it inevitably has a photo. The second feature merits one page; it seldom has a picture, so it's usually 1,250 words. And so on.

Those are the parameters that govern the length of text. An amateur writer is often unrealistic. He reads in the *Writer's Handbook* or *Writers' & Artists' Yearbook* that this magazine takes non-fiction of either 1,250 words or 2,250 – AND HE SENDS IN 3,000 WORDS.

He has reasoned (quite correctly) that his piece is just the sort of subject this readership laps up. And his journalism tutor told him it's well written.

The editor rejects it because neither he nor his staff (if he has any) can afford the time out of their killingly busy schedule to cut it to the length they said they would accept. A rewrite job can take as long as, or even longer than, writing the original piece. And, as in 99 per cent of cases, the editor doesn't have the time to write on the rejection slip *why* it can't be accepted.

This severely erodes the author's confidence in his tutor and in his own judgement. He's completely misunderstood why the feature has been rejected. So he throws in the towel and enrols for pottery classes. And possibly a promising writing talent is lost to the public.

# How to write to length as you go, rather than cut afterwards

Not writing to length is a pet gripe of editors and a frequent reason for rejection. Beginner writers can't or won't see this – they think the editor will merely cut it or add to it. Instead it'll be rejected in favour of a piece from another freelance that's the right length.

MSS aren't always rejected because they're below standard. Over-length is as big a reason.

I can't see why writers find it so difficult – just count the ruddy words, one, two, three, four. Yes, it's tedious. Tough. There's tedium in all jobs.

Invest in a word processor if you want it done for you. Some models will count the words as you're writing, others will only do it at the end of the piece.

There are two methods of getting the piece to the right length. And with beginner writers it's nearly always over-long. If it's too short, then they haven't done enough research or interviewing.

If you aren't up against a tight deadline you've time to write a first draft, then cut words when you do the second and third. The very best way here is to polish it in the second draft then PUT IT AWAY IN A DRAWER FOR A DAY OR TWO, longer if there's time. When you return to it you'll be capable of a much more objective overview and see all sorts of words you can cut further.

But let's say you're short of time. If you write for newspapers you will be. Or if, in answer to your outline letter, the editor has said: 'Yes, I like the idea and I want it on my desk the day after tomorrow,' then you'll need the first version to be to length straight off.

*This is how you do it:*

(1) Note down the target number of words.
(2) Type away. When you've done 10 or 12 lines, count the words. This is to discover how many lines equal 100 words.
(3) On your scrap paper note the first word in the line containing the 100th word. Next to it write 100.
(4) From then on you need only count lines. When you've typed another 10 or 12 lines (it varies, depending on the size of type

in your typewriter/word processor), again note down the first word in the line containing the 200th word. Next to it write the figure 200.

(5) And so on until you've reached the specified number.

This method avoids over-writing. You can see AS YOU PRO-GRESS how to tailor to length; how many words you can afford to devote to each point you're making.

## More on presentation

One reason for sending in your copy as near perfect as you can is that you're more likely to have printed what you have written.

You can't today rely on the publication using experienced type-setters who will realise you've slipped up somewhere on grammar, say, and will correct it for you. For cheapness, some publishing companies employ any kid who can vaguely find their way around a keyboard. Some haven't fully grasped printer's marks or how to visualise the final setting on the page. Neither are they always completely literate.

And note this. Submitting a photocopy of your piece is a dead turn-off. Editors will suspect you're sending the piece to other magazines, and just not bother even to read it. If it's inevitable that you send a photocopy instead of the original, mark it in large capitals 'NOT A MULTIPLE SUBMISSION'.

Do you have a typewriter? If you do, or a word processor, then great. If not, to familiarise yourself with a keyboard, second-hand manual typewriters aren't expensive. Try the classified ads in the local paper, *Loot* (if you live in London) or *Exchange & Mart*. Adult Education classes in typing are available in most boroughs. Being able to type, and type well, is an ESSENTIAL for the journalist. While you're learning, get your MSS typed by a professional, and show them my layout guidelines in Chapter 2. See your local paper's classified ads for a typist, also Yellow Pages.

# Checkpoints

*Before sending off any news story, feature, profile, review etc. check you can answer 'Yes' to all these questions:*

MARKET — is it right for the readership?

LENGTH — does it have the number of words specified?

PRESENTATION — is it typed and laid out professionally?

HEADLINE — is it short, with a verb, and not a mere label?

OPENING — does intro have impact and compel reader to read on?

ANGLE — is it original, really NEW, not been done before?

TOPICAL — do I have the very latest facts?

CLICHÉS — is the piece free of trite phrases?

QUOTES — are there plenty of them, to give lots of human interest?

SENTENCES — are they no longer than 27 words?

LANGUAGE — short words, active not passive, non-verbose?

GRAMMAR — are syntax, tenses and punctuation correct?

SPELLING — are all doubtful words checked, especially names?

ARGUMENT — is it balanced, with both sides presented?

FOCUS — have I stuck to the point and not deviated?

ENDING — does it round off the piece effectively, possibly mentioning future plans?

# Chapter 11

# News Features

- Classic news features
- For local or national Press
- Update features
- Discoveries
- Advertorials
- Profiles
- Pictorials

---

'FIVE years ago we were printing 28 pages. This year 48 – and it's still not enough. People want more words, better pictures. It's a booming industry. It's terrific.'

PETER PRESTON, Editor, *The Guardian*

---

FEATURE WRITING gives journalists the opportunity of meeting all sorts of people and visiting all sorts of places unavailable to the general public.

Pointers we've already covered apply to features, eg: openings with impact, significant endings, style, length, presentation (and I have more tips for you later). In fact, they apply equally to every piece of journalism including news stories, profiles and reviews.

News features are the pieces, longer than news stories, that appear on the centre pages of the local and national Press and in newsmagazines.

They're different from articles. Why? To start with, the best ones have QUOTES. Journalism is getting out of your chair and asking questions to get other people's opinions and quoting their answers. This gives your writing controversy.

Another aspect that distinguishes journalistic features from articles is their TOPICALITY. They're always on topics people are talking about TODAY.

Subjects for ARTICLES are usually timeless ones: history, hobbies, visits to stately homes and beauty spots, animals, flowers, DIY. None has any immediacy. They don't usually appear in newspapers.

Incidentally, they're often the first subjects tackled by beginner writers. There isn't the pressure of news features which, because they're topical, are usually wanted tomorrow, or within a few days. The types of pieces accepted by newspapers are generally those on current developments of social issues or injustices in today's headlines.

Yet another point – features have headlines, not titles. Headlines are always active, never mere labels.

And still another point – features, like all pieces of journalism, have arresting openings.

Don't be confused by the various non-fiction pieces. Those I cover in this book are the main ones – news stories, features, profiles, reviews and fillers. But one can't always be absolutely specific. There's quite a lot of overlap between them.

By the way, I can clear up a general confusion here. An editor might easily say: 'I want an article of 1,500 words', and the beginner journalist will think: 'Oh, so an article will do. I don't have to go to all the trouble of writing a topical feature.' But they'd be wrong. The word 'article' is often used in the trade in exactly the same way as 'piece' and 'work', merely to denote 'words written on paper'. Whichever term the editor uses, she or he expects you to produce a piece of journalism, ie a feature, not an essay.

Features cover a vast spectrum.

## The classic news feature

This is based on a news item.

Unlike news stories, in features it's permissible to give opinions. But only amateurs hurtle into writing their own views. Re-read the letter by Jean Silvan Evans in Chapter 4.

Always remember that the prime aim of a feature is to INFORM and ENTERTAIN the reader. But always be aware that there's a strict law of libel.

A feasible idea for the classic news feature would be a national disaster; something like a train or plane crash. But these in-depth pieces are always handled more easily by staff journalists because newspapers employ researchers and have large and comprehensive libraries set up for this purpose. The sheer practicalities of covering a national disaster makes them too big a task for the freelance.

## LOCAL PRESS

But you could well do a feature for a local paper. Here is a news story printed in my local paper. After that is the news feature that appeared the following week.

### TRAVELLERS TOLD TO GO

A crackdown on travellers is announced by Camden Council. Travellers in Camden Square and Hawley Road face eviction next week, after council solicitors rushed through a request for a court hearing.

The action follows a report from the local government Ombudsman which criticises Camden for not evicting travellers and cleaning up after them quickly.

The Chairman of the Race and Community Relations Committee says: 'The council has a policy of not criminalising travellers for occupying sites, recognising there are no legal stopping places in London. But it is also policy to evict if they move on to public open spaces.'

Complaints were received from people living in Camden Square about the health hazards they suffered from being next to the camp.

The council has issued instructions for the mess created by the travellers to be cleaned up immediately. They will continue to monitor the situation while the travellers remain.

'The council's first duty is to protect the health of adults and children living in the borough,' says the Chairman.

*Now here's the news feature:*

### RAGGLE TAGGLE KIDS ARE 'LIKE WILD ANIMALS'

'Have you come to bring us toilets?' cry the traveller children as they run round and round in rings.

The 'person who has come to bring them toilets' seems to be the only one from outside their fenced-in little inner city world they are prepared to respect.

But they are fascinated when someone dares to step into their territory. They shout abuse, then, growing brave, come closer. If you don't draw away they try to touch you. They feel your fingers for rings, your pockets for coins and your bag for holes.

Even a traveller mother, shaking her head, says: 'They are like wild animals. But what can we do without a proper site?'

The *Caravan Site Act* of 1968 says local authorities must provide sites for their traveller population – but official estimates of numbers in each borough are based on a survey done in 1958.

According to these figures, Camden has no travellers. Yet one woman says she has lived in the borough for nine years.

Without any proper sites the travellers' lives are a round of evictions.

And there are inevitable storms about the cost to resident taxpayers of cleaning up when they leave. Barnet recently paid £100,000 to clean up an abandoned site.

Camden, which operates a 'no harassment' policy, was recently ordered to pay compensation to residents who said the council had not acted quickly enough to evict travellers and clean up sites.

There are no votes in finding the solution to the problem of travellers.

One traveller woman, when asked for her side of things, said: 'It's the same old story. We are just moved from pillar to post and back again.'

And another said: 'People complain about rubbish. But why don't they give us skips? And we're being moved all the time. If we had a proper site we'd keep it clean.'

The travellers are not short of money, says a publican near the gypsy site; 'Money's not the problem with them. They take over, then suddenly one day they'll be gone. And it can take you six months to get regular customers back again.'

The travellers may live in the centre of our cities, but they operate their own society, under their own rules.

A fence of mistrust of the outside world surrounds everything they do. Like any kids, the youngsters enjoy the attention for a while – posing, posturing, pulling faces. But suddenly they grow suspicious and pelt us with a hail of missiles.

When they reach the fence, at the outside of their world, they stop running.

A good news story and news feature written by a journalist named Claire Smith for a newspaper that's since folded (gone out of business).

Notice: no adjectives, and none of her opinions in them; just straight reporting. The opinions were of people she interviewed. This way she isn't trying to influence readers, who are left to form their own opinions on the evidence Claire reports.

How did the author get the information?

For the news story she interviewed the Chairman of the Race and Community Relations Committee. For the news feature she visited the site and interviewed the travellers and a nearby publican. And for background information on the *Caravan Site Act* of 1968, she went to the public reference library.

Don't expect me to tell you exactly where in the library. The whole idea of learning how to research is for you to make your own investigations, not for me to hand you information on a plate.

## NATIONALS

Of course, a freelance *could* handle a feature on a major disaster if they took a different angle from the national Press.

You could do a FOLLOW-UP STORY. Interview people living nearby – how do they feel now it's all over? What sort of future life is there for the victims? The maimed may lose their jobs – the badly maimed *will* lose their jobs. Ask about the strain on the families who look after invalids; ask about medical help, about support groups to help people get over the shock (which can be present for months and set up psychological disorders).

There are many consequences following a disaster to provide you with unusual angles to follow up. For more questions to ask, use CIPP. This method will reveal all sorts of questions for which you need answers.

## The update news feature

This gives the reader the latest news, trends and developments on any subject you care to name. New rules announced in Parliament are pertinent triggers. For this type you need special up-to-the-minute information and your finger on the pulse of everyday happenings. Read newspapers, catch TV and radio news.

And, just as important, build up PRESS CUTTINGS files on any subject that interests you. Clip everything you read on it, make notes if it's on the box or radio. When you come to write your feature, it's all there waiting for you to weave in.

An Update News Feature is best done by people who specialise in some area and have access to the latest developments, or are in contact with someone who does.

**Example:** A nurse could write a feature on new training procedures for hospital staff following innovative methods discovered in kidney dialysis.

**Example:** A teacher could write a feature about the effects on parents and children of the latest moves in education.

A reminder on press cuttings; what do you have to do to each? If you don't ALWAYS write on each one the name of the publication and date you won't be able to ring up later to ask them for more facts, or the whereabouts of a person who's mentioned whom it's vital for you to contact.

## The discoveries news feature

This is a write-up revealing the largest, smallest, longest, shortest, fastest, whatever.

**Example:** Parsifal & Co have just brought out the smallest TV set yet known. It will fit into a matchbox! You start with a news item

you've read then enlarge on it. What are or could be the REPER-
CUSSIONS? How will it affect PEOPLE? The good old CAUSE AND
EFFECT formula: such and such has happened, so it will now be
possible to . . .

This is well within the scope of the beginner freelance journalist.

# Advertorials

This is the type of news feature that hinges on events like the
opening of a shop's second store, or a factory extending its
premises, or a business offering a new Customer Service. The
reason it's called an advertorial is because the feature will be
juxtapositioned on the same page as advertising paid for by the
company in focus.

This will inevitably be for the local or trade Press.

They are labelled something like 'Advertisement Feature' or
'Advertising Supplement'. Sometimes it's the centre spread or
centre four pages and can be a 'pull out'. In this case there will be a
great many adverts. Quite often they're paid for by neighbouring
firms wishing the focus company good luck on their new venture.

The feature will concentrate on the benefits to the general public
of the new branch, extension, service, whatever, usually through
quotes from one or more of the senior management. This will be
followed by weaving in some of the firm's background history.
Indeed, some advertorials are hung on a company's anniversary,
the 'news' being that they have traded at this address for the last
fifty years.

Advertorials aren't publicity puffs – well, the good ones aren't.
Never being able to forget that it's the advertisers that finance all
publications (so they mustn't be upset), this type of editorial
presents a real challenge to the journalist. It's important to write
an objective piece, keeping out eulogies.

This is a point you need to make when you're interviewing the
managing director, or whoever. All he'll want you to write is what
a marvellous company his is.

Possibly the germ of the idea will come from a friend employed
locally: 'My shop's opening a new branch in the High Street next

summer. With a bit of luck I'll get to work there.'

'Right', thinks you, 'There's a story here.'

Your first preliminary phone call is to the firm's boss. 'If I could swing a feature about your company in the local paper, would you be willing to back it with advertising? And if so, how much?'

If he says yes, your next call is to the editor. 'A local, well established shop (don't divulge the name, then they can't put their own reporter on the story) has a new branch opening in a few months. If I could guarantee they'd take space, would the paper accept a news feature from me?' If the editor sounds interested you then talk money:

(a) what's the minimum amount of advertising space the shop has to take?

(b) how much will you pay me?

## The people-in-the-news profile

A write-up of somebody CURRENTLY IN THE NEWS. This is pretty self-explanatory. Go out and interview the person.

Sometimes a profile doesn't need a face-to-face interview – then it's what is known as a scissors-and-paste job. This type can only be done on people who are often written about by the Press and whose biography or autobiography is in print. It's all book research. But these pieces aren't the best journalism.

The most interesting profiles are stuffed full of quotes gleaned *recently* from a live interview. Chapters 15, 16, and 17 focus on live interview techniques, and the profiles themselves.

## The pictorial

If you're good with a camera (and I mean REALLY good, not just by the occasional fluke), you can take care of quite a few of your mortgage repayments by selling the type of feature that's creatively illustrated.

A plus is that these pieces are usually large ones if you can supply a choice of, say, three dozen pix (jargon for pictures). The editor might give you a double page spread, or even more. In Sunday newspaper supplements you're talking £800 to £1,500 and up at the time of writing, excluding expenses.

Pictures *would* be high quality if you worked with a freelance photographer. But be aware of the problems of dividing the fee and secondary rights. I explain how to brief a photographer in Chapter 20.

For photo features subjects could be anything at all that's currently in the news and is VISUAL. What topics? Think VISUALLY now . . . ecology problems, threatened wildlife, a re-greening project, a large-scale disaster, unusual customs here or in a country in the headlines, recent archaeological discoveries. They would all provide exciting pictures.

But ALWAYS, ALWAYS GET THE COMMISSION BEFORE YOU TAKE THE PHOTOS. If you don't know which publication will take the feature, you won't know which type of shots their house style demands.

If it's a colour feature, that means transparencies (certainly not prints), and preferably of professional size 2¼ inches (57mm) square. If you have some *really* special pix, say action shots, the editor may relent and take 35mm slides. *If* they're top quality.

Or if the pix have to be black and white, they'll want prints (always GLOSSY, please, not matt), and they have to be taken with a black and white film in the first place.

As for the size of black/white prints, editors don't like anything smaller than either 6 inches by 6 inches (152mm × 152mm) or 5 inches by 7 inches (127mm by 177mm). It isn't necessary to send in 8 inches by 10 inches (whole plate) prints. This size is more for advertising – anyway they're expensive.

Whatever size you send, the publication's printer expects to have to reduce or enlarge them to make them fit the space allocated on the page.

As the entire amateur film processing industry has gone over to colour, getting black/white films processed rapidly can be a real headache. Or it was until the relatively recent advent of High Street processing laboratory-shops. They have one-hour, three-hour and 24-hour services. It's almost as if they knew that the acceptance of a journalist's feature can rest on whether or not the pix can be on the editor's desk by this afternoon.

These High Street processing laboratories can give you a lightning service, but remember you can use *only XP1 film*. It's made by Ilford. High Street rapid processing machines can handle any other type of black/white film but not to give a one-hour processing service. They're no more expensive than the other types of film which can't be processed in less than 24 hours. You buy XP1 films at the same place that processes them.

# Chapter 12

# More on Features

- Specialising
- Trade Press
- Industrial Press
- Markets
- Angles again
- Exercise 9

- Headlines must attract, entice, inform
- Exercise 10
- More intros with impact
- Exercise 11

'TAKE a close look at your local newspaper. There's a new market for work in today's provincial press.'

CHRIS MILLER, Features Editor, Cambridge Newspapers

HERE ARE yet more tips on how to write energetic, saleable features. But first, some pointers on where to sell them. There are hundreds and I do mean hundreds, of markets. There are all the newspapers (local, regional and national) plus their weekend newsmagazines – PLUS the women's newsmags (which I'll be covering in the next chapter).

Add to these the traditional women's market, men's market, specialist Press catering for specific careers, sports, hobbies, leisure interests, nationalities, politics and religions plus the Trade Press and Industrial Press – plus radio and foreign publications. Among those are several just waiting for YOUR contributions if you can work to a professional standard.

Don't, as a new writer, be scared of them. Don't be like most beginner non-fiction writers. Because they were weaned on school essays, they try for acceptance by amateur, literary or semi-literary magazines which pay little or nothing and have no credibility on the professional scene.

Good markets for journalists to cut their teeth on are the freebie (free of charge) newspapers. They don't pay writers much, but you do get the experience. And if they print your stuff, it's something to show other editors when they ask to see your cuttings. They have similar titles to regular newspapers so non-freebie editors won't know they're gratis unless they bother to check. And they seldom do as they haven't the time.

# Specialising

Being an all-rounder is fine. Some journalists earn a really decent income turning their hand to anything. Hail to the good old maxim 'A journalist can write 1,000 words on ANY subject'. And of course, the same basic journalistic tenets apply whatever you write about, so diversification doesn't present any particular technical difficulties.

But if you specialise you're more likely to have editors coming to you.

At the completion of this book you're on a launch pad. You have the skills to be a Jack/Jill-of-all-trades or specialise. Or do a bit of both, as I do.

What's available?

The field of educational journalism? That's a good direction for a teacher-turned-journalist. Finance? That's a natural for people in banks, building societies, accountancy. Computers? Yes, for all those frustrated programmers and analysts. Capitalise on the job you're in now.

And never, NEVER leave your job for full-time journalism until you've become REALLY established. OK, you get to the stage where you're receiving a cheque almost every week. But ask yourself 'Can I keep this up?' The cruel, cold fact is that a journalist is only as good as his last idea. Can you keep pulling ideas out of your head? People in nine-to-five jobs seldom realise the sheer precariousness of the freelance way of life. Unlike the company employee, you can never rest on your laurels (or go sick or on holiday) and still be paid. Possibly the first person to put on record the writer's eternal cash flow problem was Geoffrey Chaucer. He referred constantly to 'the author's empty purse'. And he lived in the fourteenth century. Things haven't changed.

Perhaps you're not in the sort of job where you can use your daily expertise. We all eat – how about restaurant reviewing for the gourmet-turned-journalist? We all take holidays – how about travel writing?

# Specialist bodies

Joining an association devoted to your subject is a good investment. The Society of Authors has a number of sub-groups for people such as Medical Writers, Scientific/Technical Authors and Educational Writers.

There are societies for many professions and serious pursuits – the Guild of Motoring Writers, Guild of Agricultural Journalists, Yachting Journalists' Assoc., British Guild of Travel Writers. Look at the extensive list in the *Writers' & Artists' Yearbook* and *Writer's Handbook*.

# Trade Press

If you have inside knowledge/experience, there's not too much competition for freelances in specialist publications and in the trade Press.

The trade Press is made up of a number of monthly and weekly journals from one or more competing publishers which focus on news within a particular industrial or commercial area. Some examples are: *Travel Trade Gazette, Stationery Trade Review, Architects' Review, British Medical Journal, Hotel & Caterer, Farmer's Weekly, Ironmonger's Gazette*. There are literally hundreds of them, as every trade and profession supports one or more.

Apart from a couple such as *Campaign* and *UK Press Gazette*, many are not available in newsagents but are on subscription paid direct to the publication.

Neither are they listed in the *Writers' & Artists' Yearbook* or *Writer's Handbook*. Look in *Willing's Press Guide*.

They exist mainly to help readers boost profits. Their news stories and news features cover trade fairs, product launches, improved production methods, new plant, machinery and office equipment/systems, and advertising campaigns.

Some thousands of journalists are staffers on trade publications.

# Industrial Press

There's even less freelance competition in the industrial press. But to be truthful, there are fewer opportunities.

The industrial Press is newspapers and magazines published by companies in industry for their own use. Many hundreds of professional (and not so professional) journalists work on these 'house journals'.

The staff of the best ones are members of the British Association of Industrial Editors which advocates high standards.

Their function is to report company news to the firm's own employees, shareholders and customers.

Not many, but some of the publications (those of a few of the larger companies) accept freelance contributions.

**Examples are:** *Shell News* belonging to Shell Oil, *Sesame* (Open University), *Uniview* (Unilever), *JS Journal* (Sainsburys).

They were vigorously publishing features on issues related to their industry when I last checked.

Again, you won't find them in the *Writers' & Artists' Yearbook* or the *Writer's Handbook* or in newsagents.

# Markets

Let's look at the suitability or not of features for specific markets.

**Example:** The editor of *The Times* will never take a feature on a 98-year-old man who keeps bees in East Heath Road, Hampstead. Why? Readers want NATIONAL news. But the editor of *Hampstead & Highgate Express* might well go for it.

**Example:** The London *Evening Standard* would reject a well researched and authenticated feature on the recent rapid increase in the number of cases of leukaemia in Doncaster. Why? All the readers live in London and the Home Counties and buy that newspaper so they can catch up on their own *local* news.

The same goes for magazines – that's a huge feature market.

**Example:** Do you think *Autocar* would take a piece on Shelters for Battered Women? Of course not.

**Example:** The editor of *Woman's Own* – would she look at something entitled 'Profitable Combine Harvesting'? Again, certainly not.

You laugh – but writers do make submissions as unsuitable as this, they really do; and often. Their piece is turned down for the fourth time – annihilation of hope and confidence. So blind desperation blunts their logic, and they select another market merely by sticking a pin in the first page of the *Writer's Handbook*.

A brief word about WOMEN'S MAGAZINES. All the upmarket ones and the newsmags are interested in newsy features and fillers on human problems and current events. Many journalists (men and women) make a living writing for them alone. Today, women are not, repeat NOT, only interested in clothes and babies. Housewife is now a dirty word. A recent national survey reveals: 'Three out of four British wives have outside jobs, and this figure will rise to 80 per cent in 1995.' Most of these women have interests outside the home. I cover this market in Chapter 19.

I've said this before. It's a sobering fact that often the only difference between people who are published and people who aren't is NOT a lack of talent, but a lack of marketing know-how.

## Angles again

So, having sorted out your market, don't be afraid of approaching newspapers and magazines. I wish I was with you to hold your hand, but I'm not. Just go ahead and do it. You know how to write an outline now. To build an entire house, someone has to place the first brick. If your brick is a good, saleable idea for either news or a feature, then you've a sporting chance.

As everything that exists has already been written about dozens of times, what you need is a good ANGLE. You may still not be quite clear on this. We'll do an exercise on it in a minute.

**Example:** Subject is the Olympics. The ANGLE could be 'In the light of the number of drugs now used by athletes, should the

Games be abandoned?'; or 'How many countries can afford to host one?'; or 'Should it be obligatory for athletes to wear non-sponsored clothes so there's no advertising?' There's three angles on one subject.

**Example:** Subject is Parties. The ANGLE for the *Sunday Times* could be 'The political machinations of party-giving to further the career of the breadwinner'; or, for *City Limits*, 'Who will attend a forthcoming party to support the AIDS charity Crusade?'; or, for the *Guardian* Woman's Page, 'All guests are drivers. In the light of the Don't Drink 'n Drive campaign, what drinks should I serve?'

## EXERCISE 9

A treat for you now – let's have a little practise creating angles. You can choose your own subject or select one I'll give you. Thinking on your feet – don't cheat now – give yourself exactly three minutes. Time yourself – then write down (1) the subject you've selected, (2) a saleable *angle* for today's readers.

Now, your own topic or one of the following: (a) Adult Education, or (b) Lead-free Petrol, or (c) Home Computers. You've got three minutes.

Did you manage to come up with an angle in three minutes? If you found it difficult, have another go, but this time use the CIPP method. We'll be using your angles for a later exercise.

# Headlines

A few pointers now on headlines. A golden rule: whatever you do, never delay writing the piece because you can't think of one. THE BEST 'HEADERS' COME OUT OF THE FEATURE ITSELF. It's probably the *last* thing you write.

A headline has a job to do. First, what it is NOT is a label. The most amateur way of heading a piece is to take the subject and just stick it at the top of the page – *Adult Education*, or *Lead-free Petrol*, or *Home Computers*. Labels are the words appearing at the top of reports, on files and jampots. The function of a label is merely instant identification.

The headline of a feature should identify the subject – and far more. It must:

- ATTRACT – hey, I'm here, look at me;
- ENTICE – this sounds interesting, I MUST read it;
- INFORM – subject covered, plus angle.

If your headline does all those things for the reader, the chances are they'll do the same for the editor. Believe it or not, editors are human. They're susceptible to the same psychology as readers. So initially you're trying to attract *his* attention and make *him* read the piece.

So how do you make the headline attractive, enticing and informative?

- VERB – to make it active and most likely to attract attention it needs to be active, so it must contain a verb.
- IMPACT – to entice, ensure it makes a vivid impression. Then they'll read on. Hopefully the reader will step back in amazement!
- CONCISE – so that the reader can absorb the information at a glance, it needs to be brief. The ideal is three to six words.

## Examples:

(1) *Hostage Flies Home to Freedom* (cause and effect);
(2) *Volunteers Fight Violence with Caring* (subject and angle) – this is on local support groups for first-time offenders;
(3) *Mystery Bug Attacks Schoolkids* (enticing and emotive).

Can you pick out the verbs? (flies, fight and attacks).

You'll notice all the 'headers' are mini-summaries. That's why it's far easier to compile the headline AFTER you've written the piece. Of course, just occasionally a great headline will pop into your mind which will then inspire the feature. But this is very rare.

A professional always qualifies the header in the body of the piece. It's cheating to create an enticing headline but when the editor reads the piece the point promised isn't covered in depth or at all. (Well, it wouldn't be accepted.)

## EXERCISE 10

Let's return to the three subjects I set where you had to think up angles (*Exercise 9*). You've worked out angles – can you now come up with headlines? The subjects were Adult Education, Lead-free Petrol and Home Computers.

Lean on your creativity now. As usual, do the exercise before you look up the examples at the back of the book.

# More intros with impact

OK, I've said it before – but this is one of the journalistic tenets that really is vital to success. As with intros for news stories, unless your beginning has IMPACT the feature stands little chance of being accepted. This is because it won't be journalism. It's articles that have meandering introductions. The classic opening is to start with the RESULT – the action that has been taken or is about to be taken by the person you interviewed.

**Example intros:**
'This month Prof. Mark Smith is setting up two specialist support groups in Coventry since the discovery that AIDS is on the increase there.'

'Sheffield spastic children are to get a seaside outing in June because Mary Jones raised £1,000 from a sponsored swim.'

Both hinge on NEWS. Both start straight in with the result – both cause and effect. Both give facts only, no opinion.

## EXERCISE 11

Write the opening pars of a news feature for your local paper.

The first step is to search your local newspaper for a news story which can follow up with a news feature. Step two is to write the subject of the news story in the centre of a large piece of blank paper and work out the various avenues you can explore using the CIPP method.

Before you go on to the next chapter, please go to your newsagent and buy a copy each of *Best, Take a Break*, and *Bella* (they're not very expensive). You'll also need copies of your local weekly what's-on publication. In London these include *Time Out* and *City Limits*. In addition, pick up as many different copies of weekly freebie job vacancy magazines as you can. In London these include *Nine-To-Five*, *Midweek* and *Ms London*.

# Chapter 13

# Newsmagazines

- Differences in character
- Exercise 12
- Opportunities for freelances
- Evolution of newsmags

- Freelance potential
- Comparative rates of pay
- Importance of formulas

---

'DON'T go above the head of the person doing the commissioning. Features editors don't like to feel people are foisted on them. You have to grovel to everyone.'

MARK JONES, Editor, *Campaign*

---

YOU NEED only write on everyday human problems for this market – and features can be as short as 200 words. Newsmagazines are relatively new – and they use a huge amount of material from freelances.

Do you have copies of *Best* and *Bella* plus your local What's-on-in-entertainment publications like *Time Out* and *City Limits* plus job-vacancy weekly freebies? You can't work through this chapter and the next without them.

I don't hold up newsmags as examples of great journalism. Look to the national newspapers and upmarket magazines for that. But from where the beginner journalist sits, newsmags look good as they accept features on problems met by ordinary people. These could easily be heavy difficulties you or someone you know have experienced. It's always easier to write about the familiar.

And these pieces usually need interviews with the man or

woman in the street. This isn't half as scary as it sounds, and is less
of an ordeal for the beginner than questioning 'celebrity names'.

Writing for newsmags teaches you to handle emotion convinc-
ingly. This is one of the most difficult things to put into words
without sounding slushy, mushy, maudlin or twee. When beginners write emotively they often get overkill by using too many
adjectives and adverbs.

## There's a good choice

At the time of writing, there are five newsmags aimed at women,
plus half a dozen London job vacancy newsmags. Most are
weeklies (and widely read by men, incidentally). There's also the
unisex London entertainment listings newsmags *City Limits* and
*Time Out* – all want newsy features. All take at least some of their
material from freelances.

## Differentiating publications

So that adds up to about 14 titles we can term newsmags. But the
similarity ends there. Publications are like people – all individuals.
And, as with people, they like to think they're unique enough not
to be confused with each other.

To help with your market research, let's first focus on WHY
many magazines seem to be identical.

The women's market is the largest one for freelances (and
includes lots of newsmags). I asked a private student of mine to
study it and select journals he wanted to write for.

He came back with a great pile of magazines and newsmags and
told me they were all the same.

The trap he'd fallen into was understandable, and to explain it I
need to tell you a bit about how magazines work.

## Pictures – huge reader appeal

You've very likely heard journalism's well-proven maxim, A PIC-
TURE IS WORTH A THOUSAND WORDS. My student's assessment
illustrates the point admirably.

He had been overwhelmed by the pictures – all in full colour – visually very powerful – they jump at you off the pages. Ninety per cent of them were of cosmetics, clothes and cookery – archetypal women's subjects. Can you guess why?

Every woman is interested in one or more of these subjects. Another reason, magazines receive hundreds of free photos from cosmetics, clothes and food manufacturers. In the first place it wouldn't make economic sense if the editor ignored them. Secondly, the manufacturers are also the advertisers – and no editor upsets the advertisers. That's the revenue that keeps the publication alive. It provides much more income than the cover price.

Incidentally, women's magazines aren't the only ones showered with free photos – car magazines receive them, too, so do hi-fi mags, computer mags – and many others.

What my student had discovered was that ALL magazines are product oriented.

## EXERCISE 12

Women's magazines mostly carry pix (pictures) of the 'Four Cs'. Can you guess what they are? Have a try before you look at the back of the book.

Suppliers send editors thousands of free black/white and colour photos of products they want to sell.

When you're assessing a mag with a view to writing for it, the illustrations are invaluable to determine the readership profile. The people in the pix are the types at whom the mag is aimed – same sex, same age, same levels of affluence and intellect. Take a good look at the newsmags you have.

# Opportunities for freelances

OK, so now you've worked out the reader profile – you know who you're writing for. Next you want to determine the *freelance opportunities*. But you *don't* look at the pages devoted to the Four Cs – they're almost always handled by staffers who write up the same old subjects year in and year out. This is what is known as the backbone of the publication. No, you look at all the OTHER pages. And these are the ones that are mainly responsible for the magazine's personality – its individuality. Women's newsmags and mags *are* all similar in that, because they have to be product oriented to attract the advertisers and therefore make the publication pay, they carry pix of products that appeal to women. Where they differ is in the EDITORIAL – and that's often supplied by freelances.

## The birth of newsmags

Back to newsmagazines – why did they happened at all?

Generalisations are dangerous, but to identify readership, let's look at what the vast majority of the British public usually read.

Surveys show that women buy far more mags than men. There's a female and male interest in specialist hobby and leisure titles, but, as you know, additionally there's this huge demand for mags covering women's subjects – the Four Cs. For current events women also read newspapers.

But 'twas only a few decades ago that publishers realised that newspapers are actually READ REGULARLY BY WOMEN. Ah! – a new market.

OK, OK, for the pedants I'll record here that in 1903 Northcliffe founded the *Daily Mirror* as a specifically female paper – 'By women, for women', he said. But from initial sales of 265,000 copies, within three months this had plummeted to 25,000 – the most dramatic drop in newspaper history. Even Northcliffe acknowledged it was a failure.

I'm now talking post-1903 when a trend emerged in the more upmarket newspapers to have Women's Pages. These were devoted to 'female' topics – not the Four Cs so much, but profiles, current events, and community problems particularly.

From this developed newspapers launching their own full-colour unisex mags. The quality Sundays were the first (eg the *Sunday Times Magazine* was founded in 1962) and practically every newspaper has one today.

# A new battlefield

The magazine publishers weren't too happy about any of this. Losing readers to newspapers just wasn't on. They fought back – and invented different ammunition.

They pioneered an untried type of magazine for this recently discovered phenomenon – women, and not just the brainy ones, were genuinely interested in NEWS, in current events. To tempt women readers to the innovative newsmagazines, alongside the features were their old friends the Four Cs.

First off the launch pad in 1985 was ITP's *Chat*. It was aimed at the lower end of the market – housewife mums with perhaps a part-time job in a shop or factory.

Having found a gap in the non-fiction market, *Chat* took off like a small rocket. Other magazine publishers did a bit of loin girding.

The German group G & J were the next publisher to dip a toe in the gravy. In 1987 they launched *Best* – aimed at neither the bottom nor the top end of the market, but mid-ground. What sort of women do you think were their target?

Again, some were mothers, but more important, they often had full-time jobs or careers. Their age group was 20 to 45.

By the way, although the target readers were (and still are) in the 20–45 age group, *Best* is widely read both by teenagers and women in their 50s and upwards.

But G & J weren't able to keep the impending launch of *Best* a secret. They tried hard, but they'd had a success a year before with something similar, and this alerted the publishing world. In 1986 they'd launched *Prima*, a monthly containing practical, useful and human interest features.

So, when they launched *Best* in early summer 1987, Bauer followed in October with *Bella*. This is a very similar newsmag in format, but pays freelances a higher rate.

These two have remained deadly rivals ever since: both weeklies, both aimed at the same audience.

And not to be left out, in 1989 IPC launched *Me* and Bauer created *Take a Break*.

The advent of these five newsmags: *Chat*, *Best*, *Bella*, *Me* and *Take a Break*, was one of the best things to happen to freelances since word processors.

In a different newsmag class (because it doesn't carry practical Four Cs pieces), is the weekly *Hello*, launched in 1988. Chief Sub-editor Terry Hughes told me:

'We're a family news magazine entirely dependent on photo journalism. Our main focus is on colour pictures of the rich and famous doing their thing; and these features are supplied by regular contributors.

'New writers should look at our black and white pages such as 'Panorama' and 'Double Take'. Contributors must remember that immediacy is ALL (we have a *very* short lead time), and every piece is exclusive.

'We like real life dramas, for instance, someone overcoming a severe illness or coping with a traumatic emotional situation. And, of course, the picture is most important – the text is really secondary to the illustration.'

## Freelance potential

Let's consider just two publications. *Best* and *Bella* average 70 pages each – approximately 140 pages to fill EVERY WEEK. Despite the amount of space taken by the adverts, and regular columns written by staffers, that adds up to an encouraging amount of freelance opportunities in those two newsmags alone. If you add the other three, it's getting on for 250 PAGES A WEEK between them – and there are 52 weeks in a year. Just think of that huge demand for copy.

It's important to understand the difference between newsmags and magazines. Newsmags are an easier market for beginner journalists:

(1) they take lots of very short pieces from as little as 200 words;
(2) their subjects often need interviews with ordinary people, not big names, who can be, for the inexperienced interviewer, both scary and difficult to contact.

Another publication I'll mention briefly because it can only loosely be called a newsmag – it doesn't concentrate so heavily on current news events. *More* is a fortnightly, launched in April 1988. It's aimed at a younger age group – teens to twenties. The editor told me it's a follow-on from their other publication *Just Seventeen*. Their target readers are single, are working, have no dependants, so have plenty of money to spend on themselves. They're very heavily into pop music and current pop entertainment events. So they want short, newsy pieces on these topics.

The high salaries paid to many of today's teens, twenties and thirties are a gigantic green light for publishers. They want some of this money. Many magazines are designed to siphon if off from the purses of young, single women – and their buoyant sales figures show they got their market research right.

# What do they pay?

Just look at these rates of pay. At the time of writing *Chat* gives £250 for 800 words – *Best* £100 for 400 words – *Bella* £300 for 1,000 words.

On the other hand, if you write reviews for the unisex newsmag *City Limits* you're not going to get rich. Compare this – for 150 words *Best* would pay up to £40, but the *City Limits* rate is £8. *Time Out*'s current rate is quoted at £140 per 1,000 words in the *Writers' & Artists' Yearbook*.

These are ONLY ROUGH GUIDES – rates alter with time.

And payment often varies according to your writing experience. The editor of a Sunday newspaper colour supplement told me her going rate for first-timers was £150 per 1,000 words, but she paid £500 per 1,000 to her regular freelances who had proved their professionalism.

To make a profit, publications have to pay a minimum fee for the maximum quality. And they don't rush cheques to you.

Their main revenue is from their advertisers. Check the advertising rates – if they're high the editor can afford to pay writers well. Warning: this yardstick doesn't always work out – it's merely a guideline. Work done for the upmarket *Harpers & Queen*, for example, is mostly all glory – they generally pay abysmal rates.

# Formula again

Two factors newsmags borrow from newspapers is format and formula.

As you know, all newspapers have similar formats – news at the front, sport at the back, with readers able to turn straight to the weather, TV or arts pages in their regular rag knowing they are always in the same place.

*Bella* and *Best* go even further. As I mentioned earlier, the original formula writing is news reporting. These two newsmags do the same – all their regular spots are written to a strict pattern. Not the same one as news reporting – they've devised their own.

If you want to write for these two – and they're among the best payers – it's vital you discover their formulas.

To define the formula, you need to read several editions of the newsmags and analyse them. (NB: check which publications are ordered regularly by your public library.) Re-read every one of them several times so you can recognise the 'editorial treatment' falling into a pattern.

To define the specific formula of each 'spot' (they're all different), these are some of the points to note:

(a)  count the number of words;
(b)  note down factors such as whether or not quotes are used, how many there are and if a quote always introduces the piece;
(c)  the number of people interviewed;
(d)  whether written in the first or third person;
(e)  the type of ending;
(f)  is a 'facts box' included?
(g)  does it have a picture?

One great advantage of working out the formula to which newsmag features are written – you don't ever need to be 'clever' and think up different presentations. Merely write it the way it was done last time. A great deal of thought and money has gone into establishing the formulas *Best* and *Bella* use, so that pattern, and that only, is what their editors will accept.

Newsmags really are a tremendous opportunity for freelances.

A professional makes it his business to know his market inside out – that's why he's a success. It's not possible to learn journalism by merely sitting down and reading this book, believing that as you finish the last page you emerge as a journalist. To succeed you have to put down the book when I ask you to carry out market research and similar projects such as interviewing and GO OUT AND DO IT.

# Chapter 14

# More on Newsmags

- Profile of *Best*
- Some others
- Free weeklies
- What's-on weeklies

- Watch the market
- Exercise 13
- Bogus writer's block

> '*Best* and *Bella* are new generation magazines. I suspect a lot of young women buy them because: "It's not my Mum's mag" or even: "My Nan's mag".'
>
> LIZ GLAZE, IPC Editor

To GIVE you time to take a breath and take in everything I've said so far about newsmags, I thought I'd start a new chapter here.

So, still on newsmags, it will help you enormously if you have a brief but detailed analysis of each one so you know exactly what they're in the market for. (In fact, you need a similar run-down on EVERY publication you want to write for.) This is all the information you get when you do your market research, as I outlined in Chapter 6.

To show you the type of analysis I mean, here's one on *Best*. About six months after it was launched I had a long talk with the deputy editor. So I'll pass on what she told me.


*BEST*
10th Floor, Portland House, Stag Place, London SW1E 5AU.
Tel: 071–245 8700 (you add Telex and Fax numbers)

Publisher: G & J Ltd (German)
Editor: (you add this name)
Features editor: (you add this)

Reader age group 25–45
Pay £50 for 200 words
Works eight weeks ahead
Publishes Fridays
Staff of 70, plus huge army of regular freelances. They are always on look out for OCCASIONAL FREELANCES who could become regular contributors.

FORMAT (layout): SAME EVERY WEEK; similar to finding your way around a newspaper, where weather, crossword, and sport are always in the same place.

STYLE: formularised, SAME FORMULA EVERY WEEK; study each spot in *Best*, by reading several editions.

LANGUAGE: is bright, friendly, modern, mid-market, without sensationalism, they're not in the same class as *Chat*, which is further downmarket.

CONTENT: There are publications for two types of mid-market women's readers:

(a) (traditional) want romantic fiction, gossip, how-to-make features, ie knitting, embroidery, lampshades;
(b) (newsmags, [*Best*]) want short pieces and fillers on health, politics, careers, community work, emotional problems, ie lots of INFORMATION interestingly, intelligently and briefly written.

*Opportunities in* Best *for freelances*

AROUND AND ABOUT: funny or off-beat, they like puns, 300 words plus black/white pic.

PERSONAL STORY: 850 words + two pix.

THIS WEEK'S PEOPLE: celebrities, 300 word Q&A profile plus pic, pay £400.

TRAVEL: *must* be 2,500 words. Information, NOT reminiscences. Give an impression so readers would know what types of place to expect, plus 'facts box' of places to eat and visit, plus prices, hours of admission and how to get there.

NEWS FEATURES: but keep them brief.

NEWSY IDEAS: they buy ideas; ring the features editor.

*All following done by staffers* (so DON'T do one of these for Exercise 13 or send them to *Best*):

Four 'Cs' (clothes/cooking/cosmetics/children), gardening, DIY, medical, legal, motoring, knitting, cinema, video, books, music, TV, theatre.
The editor emphasises, STUDY AT LEAST SIX EDITIONS before writing.

*Best* receives 400 MSS every week. One person reads them. It can take months, so be patient.
They prefer freelances to send an outline rather than phone.

Now, mini run-downs on freelance opportunities in four other newsmags:

*BELLA*   Freelance spots: *Report* (1,500 wds) three strong case histories; *Real Life* (1,000 wds) extraordinary events, can be TOT (triumph-over-tragedy); *Families* (1,000 wds) can be TOT but must focus on a family. *True Love* (1,000 wds) unusual real life love story. Plus several other spots – write to *Bella* asking for guidelines. *Bella*, like *Best*, started mid-market but has now gone far more down-market chasing mass sales.

*CHAT*   Freelance spots: profiles on women celebrities, especially TV stars. This newsmag also likes profiles on women who are self-employed and have unusual jobs. Additionally, they're keen on women high achievers in sport.

*TAKE A BREAK*   Freelance spots: *The Way We Were*, childhood of celebrities (STRICTLY FORMULA, same questions every time, study it); *True Life* (tearjerkers), people overcoming illness or handicap; *Beyond Belief*, eg true life haunted churches and supernatural; *Relationships* (you and your bloke), 'Can I live with his adultery/violence/drink problem?'

*ME*    Freelance spots: *Face of the Week*, celebrity profiles; *Relationships*, twosome problems, eg 'Could an affair save your marriage?'; *True to Life*, unusual real-life experiences; *Other People's Lives*, profile on really interesting/unusual people.

By the time this book is published many of these spots will have been dropped by the newsmag. It's essential to analyse *current* editions.

## Weekly job vacancy freebie newsmags

With a very similar readership are the weekly freebies financed by job vacancy ads. Titles in London include *Ms London*, *Girl About Town*, *Nine-to-Five* and *Midweek*.

These newsmags are handed out, usually in tube station ticket halls, to female commuters – to men too if they want them. They're all potentially in the job market. This factor also throws into focus the target readership – 16-to-40-year-old females earning money. The bias is towards the lower end of the age range, as they are most likely to change jobs.

These newsmags all use freelance features and pay. The editors were a bit vague when I asked them how much – £25 for a short item (how short is a piece of string?) and £100 to £200 for a long one.

They're ideal nursery slopes for beginners.

They take freelance features on practically any topic affecting today's teens and twenties.

Two examples of features in *Ms London:* 'Cherie Lunghi, The Manageress' (profile) and 'What happens in a sex therapist's clinic'.

## Weekly unisex entertainment newsmags

*Time Out*, like its rival *City Limits*, is concerned with the here and now, not history. If you've ideas on entertainment, then these are your markets for reviews, and where you can give your opinions in print. But competition is fierce, as every journalist and would-be journalist who reads a book or goes to any film, play, concert, disco or whatever sends in contributions.

Their editors also take similar pieces to the freebies. Two subjects I noted for their in-depth features on current social issues were 'dating agencies for black people' and 'The vulnerability of prostitutes to AIDS'. Other big cities have their own versions of these entertainment newsmags.

# Watch the market

I've given you a run-down on the current freelance requirements of a few newsmags. In, say, two years' time, these will be different.

Freelances must continually READ AND ANALYSE CURRENT EDITIONS. Newsmags in particular change rapidly as they exhaust ideas and come up with the new ones. Today's magazines aren't static, but are evolving. And this also applies to the more traditional women's weeklies like *Woman, Woman's Realm, Woman's Own* etc, which I cover in Chapter 19.

## EXERCISE 13

Think of an idea for a short but complete piece for *Best* or *Bella*, NOT TRAVEL OR A REVIEW, please; a *brief* piece for one of the regular spots. Remember they're NEWSmags – no history. They want current events.

They like short features where women play an important role. A male private student of mine wrote five mini-features for *Best*'s 'Woman of the Week' spot. He did pieces on a girl in an all-male cricket team; a 94-year-old woman just starting to learn algebra; a 4 foot 10 inch female tiger trainer; a woman mural artist; and a teenager trainer of shire horses.

I want you to research it, then try to write it in one sitting. Don't just write it for the newsmag generally, choose one of their SPECIFIC regular spots that uses freelance material. Remember, keep away from the Four Cs and the other subjects I mentioned that are usually handled by staffers. They write up the same old subjects season by season – the foundation of the magazine. What freelances supply is the original stuff – new and unusual slants on traditional subjects.

When it's finished, check it against the list of Checkpoints in Chapter 10. If you can answer 'yes' to all the questions, then promote it in an outline to send to *Best*'s features editor. Post off the outline, and good luck.

## Bogus writer's block

Now to something that can happen when you write for newsmags or any other market.

Have you ever got a great idea, enthusiastically researched it, then the inside of your head goes blank and you just can't get down to writing it, however much you want to? Worry ye not. It happens to us all. It's a natural process of the brain.

Not convinced? Let's look at the documented research of a group of educational psychologists. Their theory is that the process goes like this . . .

The brain has two sides – the right side deals with creativity, the left with logic.

Creativity is a five-part process:
1 Idea . . . 2 Research . . . 3 Incubation . . . 4 Realisation . . . 5 Execution.

**STEP 1 – IDEA,** is something that happens in the right side of brain, the creative side – Pow! you've this great idea for an angle. We'll say you came up with – 'the difficulties male secretaries have in finding a job'.

**STEP 2 – RESEARCH,** you switch to the left side of your brain, the logic. 'Let's see, I know Oliver's unemployed despite having 11 years' secretarial experience with a solicitor, 120 WPM shorthand and 85 WPM typing, faster on a word processor. (It's his case that gave me the idea.) Does he know any other men in the same position? I could interview them.'

Oliver telephoned two companies advertising job vacancies. He was told they were filled. So he got a female friend to ring; she was given an appointment at both places. You could interview her.

You could also interview bosses in various companies and people in job vacancy agencies. You have a really good idea developing here, so you're very enthusiastic.

**STEP 3 – INCUBATION PERIOD.**   Now comes another switch – back to the creative side of the brain. You've interviewed all those people and have their comments on tape. Still enthusiastic, you sit down at your typewriter ready to sort it all into a feature.

BUT, your thinking mechanism has failed! Nothing is happening up there! You want to get on and write, but all that's between your ears is porridge. This is commonly known as 'Writer's Block'.

It isn't. What's happening, say the psychologists, is that the right side of the brain is plumbing its own depths where your memory is stored. And not only YOUR memory, but 'race' memory and collective consciousness.

There's a hell of a lot for the brain to search. It works very much like a computer, but sometimes it's not as fast. This incubation period, this plumbing of the depths, TAKES TIME. And that's what's happening subconsciously when you think nothing at all is going on.

**STEP 4 – REALISATION.**   When it's finished probing, the right side suddenly says 'Wow!' as everything gels and it realises the solution. In other words, it sees how it's going to turn all those interviews into a coherent feature.

**STEP 5 – EXECUTION.**   Then, and only then, do your fingers start tapping the keys and your words begin to flow.

So when you're sitting there with a sheet of blank paper in your typewriter and a mind like a lump of sodden cabbage, you're not a failure, or sick, or different from any other writer. There's a whole lot going on inside your head which, given a little time, will manifest itself into a tangible feature.

This may seem a little far-fetched to some of you. But this right-side and left-side theory has been proved. In fact it was a brain surgeon, Bill Sperry, who first worked out that the brain was split into two hemispheres. At the time, he was researching the control of epilepsy. He discovered it first – and for his revelation was awarded the Nobel Prize in the 1980s.

This theory about creativity was the subsequent discovery of educational psychologists who carried Sperry's work further.

# Chapter 15

# Interviewing

- An ancient tradition
- Information as quotes
- Shorthand and tape recorders
- Interviewing for features and profiles
- Individuality
- Preparation

> 'I DO nine-tenths of the work before the interview. I've never asked anyone how many children they have or is this their third marriage – I find out before I go.'
>
> JEAN ROOK, Columnist, *Sunday Express*

DO YOU REALISE what a vital and fundamental tradition you're following when you interview people and pass on what they say? Has it ever occurred to you how ancient, how prehistoric is the art of interviewing and compiling features and profiles?

It originated pre-TV, pre-newspapers, pre-written language.

People have always thirsted for news – ever since it was vital for survival. The tangible emergence of significantly knowledgeable humans coincides with the invention of spoken language – people started communicating effectively with one another. They could pass on INFORMATION.

The need for each individual to start life in ignorance from square one reduced as the capability for verbal warning developed. People who communicated had a longer life expectancy.

'Don't go there, it's a sabre-toothed tiger's cave.' 'Don't eat that berry, my sister did and she died.' 'You can find dry twigs for firewood over that ridge.'

So developed the need for news-gatherers to take information from campfire to campfire. They had a very high standing. From this tradition eventually sprang the travelling bards and minstrels. But, of greater value, they also brought hard news told them by people they met on their travels. And these news-gatherers got their information by asking other people.

No journalist can operate without interviewing skills. Journalism is not merely non-fiction. It's a piece with pertinent QUOTES. Journalism is GOING OUT AND ASKING QUESTIONS OF OTHER PEOPLE, not merely writing from your own experiences and book research.

Interviewing is such a vast subject all on its own, I can't go into it in real depth in this book. But this chapter, and Chapters 16 and 17, cover enough for you to handle it effectively.

## Information as quotes

Interviewing is a method of getting information and quotes. You may be writing a news story, news feature, or profile. Interviewing is the classic way of getting pertinent quotes to bring your piece to life – to give it human interest. And, at bottom, the journalism readers want most is about PEOPLE.

To handle interviewing successfully and with confidence you need shorthand plus a recording machine.

## Shorthand

Everyone speaks many times faster than you can write longhand.

Apart from interviewing, shorthand is invaluable for any note-taking – at conferences, at public meetings, when listening to a radio or TV programme on a subject you want to write about. It's difficult to be a journalist without it. It's a vital professional skill and can be learnt in eight or ten weeks, depending on the system you choose.

Pitmans, which takes on average two years to learn, is far and away the best because it's the most accurate. (It's the only shorthand used by the *Hansard* writers in Parliament.) Remember, writing it down is only half of the process – just as important is *reading it back*. There is a shortened version, called PITMAN-SCRIPT, which takes only ten weeks to master.

Apply to Pitman's College, 154 Southampton Row, London WC1B 5AL. They also have local courses.

TEELINE is a popular system. It's simpler than Pitman's, but nevertheless extremely useful. It's taught at the London College of Printing as part of their journalism course. Don't apply to them for Teeline lessons, as they don't teach it separately. You have to be taking the entire course.

But Teeline is taught at some local council-run Adult Education Centres – so is Pitmanscript.

There's also SPEEDWRITING, which is taught by correspondence course.

# Recording machine

There are a number of reliable, inexpensive tape recorders on the market. You should be able to get a small, *unobtrusive* one for around £35. We're not into ghetto blasters here – it would frighten the pants off your interviewee. The smaller the machine, the less it will inhibit the person.

Do get a make with a good reputation. If it breaks down in the middle of an interview you could lose the scoop of the year. I use a Sanyo.

Look for a model that uses standard-size tape cassettes as these are cheaper to buy and more widely available than the mini versions (the machines are the same size).

Another tip on supplies – don't buy the machine unless it runs on batteries that are easily available. An obscure make could cause you problems later if you're anywhere but in a large town when your batteries run out. (NB: plenty of celebrities that need interviewing live deep in the country to get away from the limelight.)

Get a machine that operates on both mains and batteries. It's most economical for you to use the batteries when recording the interview, and mains electricity when transcribing. I'd also suggest a voice activated model.

# How to prepare

Never, NEVER go into any interview BLIND. The most successful and saleable profiles and features come out of interviews that are WELL PREPARED. I'll allow that there's an element of luck in any undertaking but, 'Fortune favours the prepared mind', said the French scientist Louis Pasteur.

Never forget that the interview is merely a means to an end – the written piece. You're in there digging for information.

Interviews are mainly for two types of journalism:

FEATURES – you interview people to get more information on the subject which is the focus of your piece. The person could be a specialist – anyone from a cardiologist to a plumber. Or they could be people with similar experiences, eg women and/or men who have all climbed Ben Nevis, witnessed a crime/disaster or who have been sexually abused by a parent.

PROFILES (mini biographies) – you interview celebrities or people who are, in some way, newsworthy.

# Profiles

What do we mean by a profile? It's a concise biography highlighting one or more interesting points in a person's life. It tells the reader what makes this person tick. Profiles are very popular with readers and that's why you'll find examples of them in nearly every newspaper, magazine and newsmag.

There are two types – *feature* and *Q & A (question and answer)*. The most difficult format is the feature, but it makes a more interesting read and gives the writer greater creative scope.

When you have decided upon which celebrity or specialist you're going to write a profile, identify your market BEFORE you write it to discover which type the editor takes. Some take only Q & A, some only feature. But then you already know about investigating the market before you write the piece.

# Individuality

As the ultimate aim is to SELL your profile, formulate questions to bring out facts that will interest the READER most. If you're interviewing a celebrity they've very likely been profiled several times before. You're determined to discover something NEW that the reader didn't already know.

Aim at discovering WHAT MAKES THIS PERSON DIFFERENT? Readers won't be interested in what they eat for breakfast. Find out what your subject DOES that's unusual – everyone's an individual – what's different about *this* person? Do they campaign for Green Peace? Are they taking an Open University course? Do they hang glide? Have they just had a facelift? Are they vegetarian and perhaps have husband/wife and children who are meat eaters? What are the problems involved and the benefits?

Ask whether your subject has a particular crusade at the moment, specific chip on the shoulder, an axe to grind. Indignation triggers great quotes. Find out their opinion on anything at all that's a current event or problem. Also try topics like job satisfaction, house prices, a current strike or environmental issues.

# Preparation

Preparation usually takes far longer than the actual interview. As interviewer, you must have the OBJECTIVE clearly in mind beforehand. You must know what information you need from the interviewee. Try to avoid having to go in cold and ask questions off the top of your head.

Professionals are always armed with a list of questions. This way they don't have to concentrate so hard on the questions, but can focus on the ANSWERS and their suitability for inclusion in the feature or profile that's to be written after. So, if the answers aren't shaping into a piece of saleable work, the interviewer asks additional questions to glean interesting answers that *can* be put in the feature or profile.

Another use for the list of questions. However experienced you become at interviewing you'll inevitably meet people who keep drifting off at a tangent or who are deliberately trying to avoid

answering. Interviewers need a list of questions to bring them back
on course.

That list is a lifeline, but sometimes there isn't time to prepare
one. Occasionally you have to handle an 'emergency'. You could
easily be at a party and be introduced to someone who'd make a
super profile or has just the nub of information you need for a
feature. But they're leaving for China in ten minutes. So you've
got to do an instant interview.

Another tip about questions. Answers consisting merely of a
straight 'yes' or 'no' are boring to put in your written piece. To
avoid this always ask open-ended questions. These always start
with one of our six old friends: Who, What, Where, Why, When
or How. The answers to these cannot be 'yes' or 'no'. Try asking
yourself questions and answering them to prove this point.

To avoid many of the agonies (and I DO mean agonies) experienced by interviewers when the batteries die on you, the tape gets
snarled up, the Biro runs out, you fill the last page of your
notebook, the tape recorder breaks down, your voice seizes up,
and you sit there busting to use the loo. Go equipped with spare
batteries, tapes, Biros, notebooks, tape recorder, and throat pas-
tilles – and go to the loo immediately before leaving home.

And a final contingency. Cars, buses and trains are all subject to
unexpected delays such as breakdowns and traffic jams. So you
sometimes need to ring your interviewee on your way to them to
apologise and explain that you will be late. Always take a
Phonecard and plenty of change for a public telephone.

# Chapter 16

# At the Interview

- Being in control
- Listen to the answers
- Twenty tips
- Transcripts
- Openings
- Don't let them see it
- Practise
- Exercise 14

> 'AT the end of each writing day I always leave some of
> what I've written to be typed in the morning. That way
> I never have to "start cold".'
>
> MONICA DICKENS, Novelist and ex-journalist

IF you come away from an interview without enough details for
the feature or profile you have to write, then you've failed.

## Being in control – role playing

Being in control is vital to the success of your interview and, of
course, the final written piece. Much of it is role-playing.

Your very demeanour 'takes charge' of the situation if you emit
amiable confidence. Your body language shows your interviewee
that you know what to do and he can safely leave everything in
your hands. It's important to establish this atmosphere as soon as
you arrive. It's nothing to do with being cocky or arrogant, just
quietly confident (even if you don't feel it).

From your demeanour your subject then has confidence that
'she obviously knows what she's doing' and psychologically
they'll let you take charge.

If you greet them all of a nervous twitter, vague and hesitant, they're not going to have any faith in your ability. This will make them nervous and their reaction will be: 'Well, she's a bit of a twit. One of us had better know what they're doing,' and your interviewee will slip into the role of leader.

Don't let the words 'role play' throw you. We all do it in everyday life. You visit the doctor. This is a meeting of two people where you both automatically fall into roles. You present your problem and he tries to solve it. You both expect this, so the interview goes smoothly. You both know that the doctor won't tell the patient his medical troubles, also that the patient won't advise the doctor to 'go home and rest in bed', in other words, act out of role. Much of the success of the meeting depends on both parties playing their expected roles.

And the same goes for the journalist going to an interview. Just as the patient expects the doctor to be in charge of the situation, the interviewee expects the journalist to be in charge – and will co-operate. Remember, the only way you can extract the information you want is to have a co-operative subject.

## Listen to the answers

It's very easy, while asking questions, to focus on the 'asking' while doggedly ploughing through the list of questions you've prepared. You must be concurrently thinking of the 'writing' that follows – thinking on two levels at once.

The creative part of interviewing is to formulate the structure of the text in your mind at the same time you are asking the questions – to visualise how the final piece will 'read'. Otherwise you could emerge from the interview with many answers which can't be used in your write-up or, if used, will negate its effect. Remember, you go into the interview not knowing what the person is going to say.

**Example:** You are interviewing a tutor about proposed cuts in the Adult Education budget.

Q 'How could this affect you? I understand many tutors could be without a job.'

A 'It wouldn't really matter – I have a private income.'

In print, that would weaken your write-up, which is aimed at bringing out the dire consequences of the financial cuts. You don't want answers like that. So your next question is:

Q 'How many colleagues do you have whom this will affect adversely?'
A 'Several.'
Q 'Who in particular?'
A 'Well there's Jane. She's a single mum and tutoring is her only form of income. If she lost her job she and her baby would be in serious trouble. And there's Malcolm. He barely keeps his head above water with a heavy mortgage. As he has an invalid wife who can't work all the financial responsibilities fall on his shoulders.'

And there you have some genuine cases of potential hardship which will interest the reader. You wouldn't have had these if you hadn't pursued that first question from a slightly different angle after you'd had a humdrum answer.

This is why you don't always press ahead blindly and ask the next question on your list. It's imperative that you LISTEN TO THE ANSWER, mentally assessing its value to the finished piece. After each answer you have two choices: (a) to ask the next question on your list, or (b) to pursue the previous question, but taking a different approach.

Avoid the classic situation where the interviewer sticks doggedly to his list of prepared questions, irrespective of the answers he's receiving:

Q 'So your next novel comes out in May?'
A 'Not now. It was scheduled for May but I murdured my wife.'
Q 'So *when* will your book be published?'

# Twenty tips

1 A useful move after you've asked:'What do you like about your job?' is to follow with: 'What do you hate about it?' People love to have a good old whinge – discussing their hates can be enormously revealing.

2   Another revealing question is 'What do you see yourself
    doing five years from now?'

3   A tip on being in control. That 'JAW-ME-DEAD', the person
    who won't stop talking: one way to stop them in their tracks,
    is to ask when they pause for breath, 'How much were you
    paid for your last film, or play, or book?' This will make them
    sit and think. It's curious that people will talk about terminal
    illness, death and sex, but when it comes to MONEY . . . that's
    taboo.

4   If the person is not articulating well, you can always put a
    good quote into their mouth by prompting them with:
    'Would you say that . . .?'

5   Avoid multiple questions. Suppose I asked you: 'Where were
    you born, how long did you live there, are your parents from
    the same area?' You'd be thoroughly confused. Ask ques-
    tions ONE AT A TIME.

6   Take with you more questions than you need:
    (a) your subject could be taciturn, so the answers will be
    shorter than you expect;
    (b) the interview may run over the time originally agreed,
    perhaps because it's going so well the subject gets really
    enthusiastic and is revealing like mad and not watching the
    clock.

7   Take enough questions for more than one write-up. Work out
    beforehand how many separate profiles and features you can
    get out of the one interview. In other words, how many
    different angles.

8   Taboos: unless it's specifically relevant to the piece you're
    writing, DON'T ask them their AGE or their WEIGHT. They'll
    usually lie – especially women.

9   Don't talk too much. In an ideal interview your subject talks
    for about 85 per cent of the time and you only 15 per cent.

10  A little knowledge is a dangerous thing. Don't pretend
    knowledge of your interviewee's speciality that you don't
    have, just to appear intelligent. Otherwise they won't explain

the basics that you'll need to understand their discourse. They will also use esoteric jargon.

11  Make absolutely certain at the time that you UNDERSTAND THE ANSWERS. It's very unprofessional to have to phone afterwards and clarify.

12  And on your part – do use language your subject can understand. Don't try and impress with your erudition as they could be too embarrassed to ask what you mean and will clam up on you or keep saying: 'I don't know.'

13  Sure ways of making your interviewee hostile and unco-operative are to be superior or ironic. Another way is to be impertinent – eg: 'Are you married to the man you live with?' Use diplomacy on this type of question (if it's necessary to know 'intimate' details at all).

14  A word you should use often is 'why?' – try to remember that. This word also gets you out of the hole you get yourself in if you ask a closed-end question where they answer with a bald 'no' or 'yes'. Immediately follow up with: 'Why?' And, if it's relevant, keep asking: 'Why?' to every answer that follows.

15  Don't waste time asking questions that won't get you the information you need. Something as huge and obscure as: 'What is the meaning of life?' will probably give you only waffle.

16  Don't bore your subject with lots of petty questions such as: 'What's your favourite colour?' 'What's your favourite food?' Unless the answers are directly relevant to the angle you're going to write up, this kind of information will also bore the reader.

17  Try to make the interview as casual, relaxed and close to a social conversation as possible. This will allay your subject's nervousness. But don't do what I did when I was wet behind the ears. I carried out what I thought was a very successful interview with a best-selling novelist. He wasn't nervous or put off by anything I asked, and was articulating freely.

Then came the crunch – I'm sitting in front of my typewriter to transcribe the tape. I discovered I knew masses about the performance of his car, how long it took to get from zero to 70 mph, how much it did to the gallon, why leather is a superior seat covering, how fashionable was its colour . . . BUT I didn't know how long he'd taken to write his bestseller, what motivated him to write it or what problems he'd had with the plot!

18  Don't be afraid of INTERRUPTING your subject if they're not giving you the info you want. The interviewer must BE IN CONTROL at all times.

19  The person's speciality may not interest you – but newspaper reporters can be sent to interview ANYONE on ANY subject. Force yourself to be interested in what they say.

20  DON'T BE SHY ABOUT ASKING QUESTIONS. We're brought up not to probe others as if they were at an inquisition. And that's right in a normal, social context. But interviewing is an entirely different situation. Interviewer and subject have met for no other reason than that one will question and the other will answer. The subject has agreed and expects questions – even pretty direct ones to a certain extent (which doesn't mean you can ask about their sex life!). They'll tell you if you get out of bounds. Respect them.

## Transcripts

Always type your transcript in double-line spacing because you'll need to scribble inserts all over it.

Once you've transcribed your tape on to the typewriter or word processor the resulting hard copy can be a bit daunting. A mere hour's interview can result in perhaps five typed pages. This is something like 4,500 words – and your finished piece has to be only 1,000!

The first step is to go through and underline in red the passages you will use. Often there will be far more than you need, so this is another analysis process. Highlight only the 'strong' stuff, the really pertinent statements that will make your piece stand out from all the rest. Ignore the 'ums' and 'ers' and repetitions.

A colleague of mind finds it helps to go through with different coloured felt-tips. For example, he highlights all references to childhood in green, to career in blue, to marriage in orange, to the war years in mauve, etc.

Being a professional, there'll be more than one piece you can write from the one interview. Say it's a profile; perhaps the first piece will be on the childhood and schooldays of Gloria Superstar. The quotes she made on meeting Bob Megastar you can highlight in a different colour to use in a separate feature or profile for a different market.

# Openings

When you write up any profile or feature the introductory sentence must have – WHAT? Yes, IMPACT. It applies equally to pieces of 2,000 words and 200 words.

If you're writing a profile of a person who isn't a glamorous superstar (or even if you are), start with something the person has done that is significant or dramatic. Please don't reveal your amateurism with an opening like 'Jane Brown is 22 and was born in London.' Can't you hear the reader saying: 'So what – that applies to 70,000 other people too.'

**Examples:** 'Peter Hapwood is frank about his journalistic ambitions: "I want fame. Anything Kilroy-Silk or Bernard Levin can do, I can"'; or 'Mary Dawson thinks castration is not the answer to reducing rape'; or 'Mike Blenkinson came to London for training; his aim – his first million as a Computer Programmer by the end of two years.' Use your CREATIVITY.

If you're profiling a celebrity, research pieces already written about them so you'll be able to avoid being unprofessional and asking basic questions such as 'Are you married?' and 'How many films have you made?'

When writing a feature you may have interviewed a specialist on the subject. Start your piece with the most riveting statement they made. Beginning straight off with a quote is very effective.

**Example:** 'My team spent two years of seven-day-weeks before we uncovered this virus which has killed 2,000 people,' said Peter Dexter, Consultant Microbiologist at St Mary's Hospital.

Or perhaps you didn't have to interview a specialist. Let's say the feature is about the difficulties male secretaries have in getting jobs (see Chapter 14). You could start: '"I have 11 years' secretarial experience, my shorthand is 120 WPM and I'm in my early 30s. But I can't get a job." Oliver's problem is that he isn't female.' That takes the reader straight into what the feature's about in a positive, concise and very 'human' way. The language is vivific – it lives.

NB: don't forget, in your final written piece you can't put into quotes anything the subject didn't actually say. They can sue you for misrepresentation.

## Don't let them see it

Don't, don't undermine your credibility as a journalist by agreeing to let ANYONE BUT THE EDITOR see either your transcript or the finished piece.

If you let your interviewee see either, you're invariably in for trouble. They will often ask to. So be prepared and parry with a very firm: 'Sorry, it's not journalistic policy. You must please trust my professional integrity not to libel you or present you in an unfavourable light. I don't write for the gutter press.'

If they do see what you've written before publication I guarantee they'll change it. And they'll usually delete, or reduce the impact of, the most interesting quotes, so you've lost their spontaneity.

And they won't return it for ages, often making you miss your deadline.

If they insist, try a compromise. Say you'll read it to them over the phone. Then, at least, if they demand alterations ('or I'll sue you') you can make them there and then, so you won't miss the deadline and anger your editor.

The only exception is when you've interviewed a specialist. You will earn Brownie points if you can tell your editor that the piece has been checked for accuracy.

# Practise

There's no substitute for experience. If you're suddenly faced with interviewing a stranger the mere idea can throw you severely and you could make a complete hash of it. So first practise interviewing your friends and anyone who will agree.

Also let them interview you. Being on the receiving end of an interview is valuable experience. You then know how it feels and, hopefully, this can help you put your subject at ease and shape how you ask your questions.

## EXERCISE 14

Find someone on whom you can practise interviewing. Agree a time and place CONVENIENT TO THEM. Then, work out a list of questions to ask on your Story Lead form. This is a 'role play' situation, but to get something of value from the exercise it's up to you to convince them you're serious. Confide to them that it's to help your future career.

It's important that you then write up a short profile of your subject and give it to them to read. That's the 'carrot'. Most people would be flattered and willing to let you interview them.

And, imperative this, ask them if you've reported what they said ACCURATELY. You mustn't write what they didn't say.

The more you do this exercise, the more proficient and confident you'll become.

# Chapter 17

# Profiles

'OF the many different types of writing in magazines and newspapers today, the interview or profile is probably the most saleable.'

SUSAN KING, Freelance Journalist, *Sunday Times*

IN THE LAST CHAPTER we looked at interviewing in general. In this one we're going into the technique in more detail.

For one of the courses I run, I bring in Stan Nicholls who specialises in profiles – he's written thousands. This chapter passes on the useful tips he gives.

He's an extremely versatile journalist, much published in the national Press and in magazines. He's also a tutor in Creative Writing at London's City University.

What we have, in effect, is me interviewing Stan. At the end of this chapter there's a profile he wrote of the author Al Davison in the *Guardian*.

*Joan:* Stan, you've interviewed and written profiles of several hundred people in the news. Let's start from square one: How do you get hold of these people, and what comes first, the interview or the market?

135

*Stan:* If you're just starting out as a journalist the best policy is to be truthful. Ring the person you've selected and say: 'I'm a freelance journalist, I feel I can secure a market for a profile of you. Please will you grant me an interview, at a convenient time?' You can't be specific about the actual publication at this stage.

Then, having got an appointment for your interview fixed, you go away and research your market seriously. Pinpoint two or three publications which you know print profiles of the type of person you've selected. You need more than one in case the first one isn't interested in your proposal. Ring up the features editor of the most likely publication and say: 'I've an appointment to interview X, would you be interested in 1,500 words on them?'

## Which markets?

*Joan:* Which editors are in the market for profiles?
*Stan:* This is determined very much by the interview subject. I've got to the point where I do very, very little on spec. I'm sometimes approached by the interview subject themselves. But usually I'm contacted by publishers, publicists, film distribution companies or by film makers.

## Preparation

*Joan:* How do you prepare for an interview?
*Stan:* Get to know your subject, find out before the interview all you can about them and their work, and go along with more questions than you need to ask.

For example, a publicist rang me and asked if I'd be prepared to interview Al Davison, an author born with severe spina bifida. Now 29, all his life people have told him he's a vegetable and useless. He's written his autobiography in the form of what these days is called a graphic novel – a book-length comic strip.

In this case, to prepare, I first contacted my markets and got a number of editors interested in the profile. Then I rang the author's publicist who sent me a proof copy of the book.

I discover it's good – very good. It's not being published out of pity. It's insightful, very moving, very funny. Al Davison lays out all the prejudices – the 'does he take sugar' syndrome. He's suffered that all his life. Now he's suddenly got a promising career as a comic writer and illustrator.

In this case the autobiography is the first major thing he's had published, so preparation comes down to trying as best as possible to make oneself familiar with his disability, so you can ask credible questions. But bearing in mind all the time that's just for background, as the profile is about his creative work and the autobiography.

As I read his book I made notes of questions to ask. At the same time I compiled a brief synopsis. So I end up with the story of his life, in 300 to 400 words.

Then I put the questions into chronological order before I did the actual interview. This is important. If you ask questions chronologically, it's much easier for you when you come to transcribe. You're not necessarily going to write the profile chronologically – that could be boring – but it helps your thought process flow when you're doing the first draft.

And do compile plenty of questions. You could have a difficult interviewee who doesn't do much talking but only replies in monosyllables.

As I've been doing this for a number of years, at a push I can wing it. I can go along with nothing but a tape machine and just do it. But I don't like doing that – and don't advise it, especially for beginners. It's very easy to forget vital questions. Something that would be enormously obvious on paper, wouldn't be in the heat of the conversation. So I like to take a script, even if I never refer to it. It's a type of security blanket.

# Problems

*Joan:* Do you have any hair-raising stories of problems you've met at interviews?

*Stan:* Horrors? I've done so many interviews, I must have run into almost everything that can possibly go wrong.

I've had interviews where all the person would say was 'yes' and 'no'. The way around that is to present them with propositions like: 'Would you say that . . .' Anything to get them to agree.

When you write up the profile you put those words into their mouth. It's justifiable journalism. It's not going to be a very exciting piece if it just consists of 'yes' and 'no'. Another tip is to ask open-ended questions.

I've had the interviewee's wife come in and take over – 'What he thinks is . . .' – 'No, he doesn't mean that at all . . .' – 'You go and make a cup of tea, dear, and I'll tell the man about it.'

That situation is very difficult diplomatically. One way around it is to tell his wife how charmed you are with the tea and cakes, and how interesting her comments are, but the editor really sent you for an interview with her husband and is going to be very angry if you return without one.

I've had interviews where there have been, shall we say, acts of God. Once, parts of the building collapsed while I was interviewing! I've also interviewed sitting next to a cage full of song birds. They didn't sound very loud when I was speaking to my subject, but it was all I could hear when I played back the tape.

I once conducted a 2½-hour interview where the tape turned out to be blank. A lesson there is always to test your tape before you go to make sure it's not faulty.

Another horrendous situation was where I became totally engrossed. For five hours the two of us just talked ourselves out, having a great time. I had a stack of blank tapes. But what I actually did was, when it came to the end of the side, I turned the same tape over and over! All I came away with was the last hour.

## The write-up

*Joan:* What about writing it up afterwards? What tips can you give us?

*Stan:* The actual interview is about five per cent of the job. The real work is making sense of what people say. As you know, nobody speaks neatly or entirely grammatically. Nobody puts in full stops, semi-colons or other punctuation when they're speaking. *You* have to do that.

When transcribing you can take out several hundred 'ers', 'you knows' and 'actuallys'. That sort of thing: 'Actually I've just finished the book, and actually, it's actually the best thing I've ever done.' People don't hear themselves saying it, but we all do it to one extent or another.

When you play back the tape it usually sounds absolutely terrible. The really creative element is your written interpretation of what you've recorded.

## Sell it several times

*Joan:* Both you and I were printed in the *Guardian* not too long back. My feature was the THIRD piece I got from a single interview with a Cambridge Professor of Pharmacology. This doesn't happen as an afterthought, does it, Stan? It needs pre-planning – also a knowledge of markets.

*Stan:* Yes. It would be a waste of material not to. Always try and exploit your market as much as you can. It's quite a rare interview that has only one market – quite apart from foreign publications. For instance, I do re-treads of quite a lot of my stuff for the American market and vice versa.

And the interview you do today can be the forerunner of others. Having established contact with Al Davison, in another year I can go back and say, 'Hello Al, remember me . . .?' and we can do another profile or profiles from different angles.

But from the first interview I did on him I got four sales. It was rather a special case – the first was an exclusive for a national newspaper, so no other paper would have it that week – that was part of the deal. Ethics dictate that you wouldn't sell the *Telegraph*, *Independent* and *Guardian* the same thing. You'd never work again. If you think you can get away with it, you're nuts. They all know what's going on in each other's papers.

As for the other three sales – they were all different – all tailored for the individual markets. I saw Al Davison for a couple of hours and from that tape I got four DIFFERENT pieces. It is possible they all contained one or two of the most interesting quotes, but that's all. One was very much angled to the national, another to a specialist magazine, one to disability audiences and one to an readership of new writers.

I'm talking about a daily, a weekly and two monthlies. That's another aspect you must take into account – they have different readerships, so aren't rivals.

## Specialising

*Joan:* Would you say there was any advantage in specialising?
*Stan:* It's always a good idea to have a niche for yourself in certain areas. This gives you a bit of an edge over everybody else. I tend to concentrate on doing authors and people in the film business.

Something else I do to give me an edge over the opposition is provide illustrations, such as photos of my interviewees. These aren't shots I take myself. If you ask publicists and film distribution companies they'll supply you with black and white portraits. And it saves the magazine having to go to the trouble of finding their own. This gives you a slight advantage.

You've got to remember that being a freelance is an extremely competitive way of trying to earn a living. Anything that can give you an edge over anyone else, DO it. With me it's pictures.

## Exclusives

*Joan:* A word editors receive with kisses is EXCLUSIVE. Would you say this is a sure-fire seller?
*Stan:* Certainly. If you can engineer an interview with a famous name who's never given one before, then editors will clamour for it.

By the way, there's a common misconception about the word 'exclusive' in this context. When you approach an editor with an exclusive you are offering the very FIRST opportunity to publish your piece, you're not offering him the ONLY opportunity. After you've sold your exclusive angle to a publication, you then have carte blanche to write up the piece from a different angle and sell it to another editor.

And don't forget to tell the editor *in the first sentence of your outline* that you're offering an exclusive.

# EXERCISE 15

Discover someone who is, or will be, 'in the news'. Make an appointment to interview them, get an editor interested, do the interview, write up the profile. This is a real situation now, not an academic exercise.

On pages 142–3 is Stan Nicholls' profile of Al Davison.

# The comic strip hero drawn from real life

Al Davison, a spina bifida sufferer who fought back and fought through, has found an unusual and grabby way to tell his story. **Stan Nicholls** reports

FIGHTING violent prejudice and doctors who wrote him off became a way of life for Al Davison. He had 21 operations for severe spina bifida before he was eight, but went on to confound everyone's expectations by becoming an artist and writer, a playwright, martial arts student and Buddhist. Now, he has written and illustrated his autobiography in comic strip form, *The Spiral Cage*.

When he was born 28 years ago there was little professional help available. "They tried influencing my mother against keeping me. They thought there was no hope and I should be allowed to die. As a child, people talked to the person with me, assuming I was unable to understand. When I got onto the streets I experienced a lot of abuse; stones thrown and physical attacks. My reaction was to try to fight back. I couldn't run, so I didn't have much choice."

Spina bifida sufferers are born with incomplete vertebrae at the base of their spine. This can be manifest as a lump or, in Al's case, an open wound. "They had to graft bone on to the spine to complete the vertebrae, then graft skin to cover it," he explains. "That was the initial operation. If they hadn't done it, I would have died.

"Next, they had to straighten my legs. To change the shape you have to do the operations at an early age when the bones are soft. At that stage I didn't have any expectations of walking, and throughout my childhood the doctors said it was impossible.

"But whenever I saw television I always liked the dancers and gymnasts—the more physically difficult it looked the more I wanted to do it. Being trapped in a wheelchair gave me the incentive to work on changing my life."

An early interest in art had him copying paintings by Da Vinci and Michelangelo. Then his parents introduced him to Superman.

"All I knew about him was he could fly, and he changed in a tele-phone box. So I'd get my parents to dress me in a Superman costume and go to a phone box in my wheelchair."

As a teenager, he determined to do without the chair, and eventually graduated to calliper splints. A few years ago he was able to throw these away too, and now walks unaided, although with difficulty. He studied martial arts, to defend himself against the constant harassment he faced.

In his native Newcastle he used

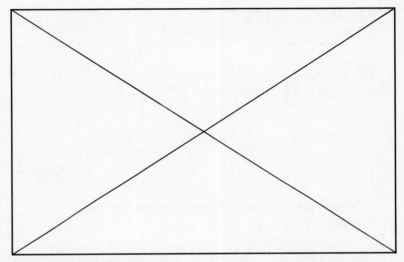

**Al Davison, defender of the faith**

PHOTOGRAPH: RICHARD RAYNER

these skills when he was attacked by skinheads who thought they had an easy target. "There were five of them—I put three in hospital."

Later he met one of his attackers. "I realised his only means of expression was violence. He was so frustrated, he had no other way of communicating. Attacking me was like smashing a mirror; he saw aspects of himself in me, and couldn't cope with it. I've found this attitude is common with people who attack the disabled.

"He said that when he got out of hospital he stopped attacking people; he'd vandalise a phone box or bus stop instead. But he also told me that when the other two got out they beat up somebody in a wheelchair."

When he discovered Buddhism he came to understand karma, the theory that every cause has an effect. "You can transmit 'victim' the same way you can make dogs sense fear. If you develop self-confidence, and the belief that you can control your environment, you're less likely to be challenged. The more confident I become the less I get attacked."

He is having his first romantic relationship, and has been with his girlfriend Maggie for a year. "Previously I went through a lot of negative feelings because women were scared of my disability. In the *Spiral Cage* I depict being attracted to women who only wanted to be friends. I was suffering, trapped in rejection, but my self-image has changed now and I can tackle this."

Something else the pair are having to tackle is the prejudice of people who cannot understand why an able-bodied woman would want to associate with a disabled man.

But he isn't depressed by these experiences. His next project is another graphic novel, and possibly a play, about his great aunt, Emily Davison, the suffragette who died under the king's horse during the 1921 Derby.

*The Spiral Cage, Titan Books, £5.95, published April 23.*

# Chapter 18

# Being Paid

- Accounting explained
- Some solutions for late payment
- Invoices
- Record-keeping
- Tax-allowable expenses

> 'WHEN a publisher is delaying payment, don't wait. Send a reminder, follow with a phone call, then if you still haven't been paid, ask us to act. We will fire off a letter to them. A single warning shot across their bows is enough.'
>
> BOB NORRIS, NUJ Legal Office

THE GOOD NEWS is that a freelance's earning potential is greater than that of a staffer. A well established freelance can become a household name and afford a glitzy, glamorous life-style, if that's what they hanker for. On the other hand they can afford a quiet, country hideaway.

If you don't reach household name status, you can still be in a very comfortable income bracket – PROVIDED YOU GET PAID.

The bad news is that when it comes to payment you have to be prepared to WAIT. It doesn't appear as a regular end-of-the-month cheque.

Freelance writers who live by their pens pay the rent with money from work they did months, even a year before. Editors and publishers are distressingly slow payers. Hardly any pay on ACCEPTANCE – most pay on PUBLICATION. In the case of a monthly or quarterly this could easily be the following year.

The fastest payers are the daily national Press who use your work within days because of its topicality. But, as with any business, they usually won't pay till the end of the following month. And sometimes the writer has to chase them.

Year in, year out, the courts are crowded with small businesses going bankrupt. All too often the reason is that they can't get their hands on money that's owed to them. In 1992 small businesses in London alone were owed a staggering £10 billion by slow payers. Freelance journalists are small businesses.

Editors have writers in a cleft stick – especially beginners. They exploit your pitiful vulnerability – and gratitude. They know newcomers are ruddy grateful to be accepted at all. And in that position of weakness they hesitate to press for payment in case they are thought 'difficult' and aren't accepted again.

But you shouldn't be grovelling. Gratitude doesn't come into it. You've worked hard, done a good job, and earned payment.

They never rush cheques to you. But if you're not paid within six weeks of publication, don't be shy of chasing their ACCOUNTS department. You don't necessarily have to speak to the editor.

If they still drag their feet, 'water dripping on the stone' is the best method. A persistent and regular barrage of phone calls and/or letters will usually get results.

Another tip if they're non-forthcoming (provided you don't live too far from them), is to ring and say: 'I'm in your area on Tuesday afternoon, I'll drop in and pick up the cheque.' That should jolt them into action.

## Accounting explained

The accounting system (cash expenditure) for every business works like this:

(1) buyer orders goods,
(2) supplier sends goods,
(3) supplier sends invoice to remind buyer to pay,
(4) buyer pays at the end of the month following receipt of goods.

Commerce recognises that the buyer keeps his money in the bank for as long as possible, where it's accruing interest for him.

Publishing uses the same system. The goods it orders from you is words.

*Sometimes the journalist will be paid* BEFORE *the end of the following month, when:*

- The editor pays on acceptance (rare).
- You've been printed by a daily newspaper.
- You have a special agreement with the editor.
- You have a special agreement with the Accounts Dept.
- The moon is blue.

*Sometimes the journalist will be paid* AFTER *the end of the following month, when:*

- The editor forgot to pass your invoice to Accounts.
- The editor forgot how much he agreed to pay you.
- The editor is on holiday.
- The Post Office didn't deliver your invoice.
- You didn't send an invoice.
- You sent a handwritten/indecipherable invoice.
- You sent an invoice showing an amount not agreed with the editor.
- Your invoice didn't state all the terms I give in my example here.
- The magazine has exceeded its monthly budget.
- The accountant doesn't want to part with the money.
- The accountant is on holiday so can't sign cheques.
- Their computer has 'gone down' (again).
- When you agreed the commission on the phone you didn't immediately send the editor a letter in duplicate confirming it, so the editor could sign and return the second copy.
- *or*, you sent a single letter of confirmation but forgot to ask the editor to confirm by fax/telex.
- They didn't use your piece, though they promised on the phone they would.
- They didn't use it, and as it was topical you can't sell it elsewhere, and the magazine doesn't have a written policy on kill fees (a fee for 'killing' your piece by not using it when they said they would).
- They didn't use it and you forgot to agree a kill fee when you got the commission.

- They printed it, but in a later edition than the one they said they would.
- They're stock-piling your piece.
- You've not reminded them (several times) that payment is overdue.
- You've lost track of where you sent your piece so you can't remind them.
- You reminded the wrong publication.
- You forgot to put your name/address on the MS.
- You put a pseudonym on your MS and forgot to add your real name, which is the one that has to go on the cheque.
- The magazine's advertisers haven't paid up so there's no money in their kitty.
- The editor has left.
- The features editor who commissioned you has left.
- The magazine is in the hands of the receiver.
- If they pay you by direct transfer, they've lost/misquoted the name of your bank/sort code.
- You are a lone freelance with no 'collective muscle'.

## Some solutions for late payment

(1) If you get no action after two reminders that payment is overdue, ring the publisher who owns the magazine.

(2) Visit the editor and accountant (take with you at least three children under school age, even borrowed ones).

(3) Gang up with colleagues who are owed money by the same publication and visit the editor *en masse*.

(4) Phone to say you'll be calling personally tomorrow to pick up your cheque.

(5) Phone/write, to say you'll take them to the Small Claims Court if the cheque isn't in your hands within four days.

(6) Get the National Union of Journalists on to them (see quote heading this chapter). NB: you have to be a member. You can't join unless 75 per cent of your income is from writing.

(7) Read Malcolm Bird's excellent book *How to Collect the Money You are Owed*. It has 124 pages of good advice, clearly explained, on action to take with or without a solicitor.

**JOAN M. CLAYTON, MAIE**
Journalist and
Graphics Designer

27 Mortimer Road,
London WW3 1ZQ
**Phone:** 071-234 5678

<u>Invoice No:</u>  27     <u>Date</u>  11 JUNE 1990

<u>Client</u>  EVENING STANDARD,
2 DERRY STREET,
LONDON W8.

To:  1,000 WORD FEATURE
"UNDERGROUND HOOLIGANS"
FOR 19 JUNE EDITION

£118·00

Payment is within 30 days of receipt of this invoice.

Interest will be charged at ten per cent per month on overdue payment.

First British Serial Rights only.

Rights of publication are author's until full payment is received.

Payment must be made whether magazine is published or not.

It is assumed the above terms are acceptable unless objections are
received in writing within seven days of the date of this invoice.

# Invoices

Make sure you send an invoice with, or immediately after, every piece you sell (you will have agreed a fee with the editor). This way you have a useful and legal record of what you're charging and what you're owed. Always type it in duplicate so you have a copy.

Opposite is the simple, straightforward invoice layout I use. Type yourself a good, black master then run off blank copies on a photocopier.

# Records are essential

Professionals keep an ACCURATE WRITTEN ACCOUNT of every MS they send out. Do it from the very first one you submit. This way you can easily check on payments and chase debtors.

I have an extremely easy system I've used all my life. One book lasts years and years, so it's not an expensive exercise. It's essential to rule pages into columns. I show you on the next page how I do my own.

If you use my method, any accountant will be able to follow it. You do know that every payment has to be DECLARED to the Inland Revenue, don't you? Don't think you can get away with it. For tax purposes every editor and publisher is legally bound to declare to the Inland Revenue all payments made to writers, so they already know about you.

Another essential where my records system is a help – you know WHERE all your MSS are. No writer worth their salt produces one work, sends it off, then waits till it's accepted/rejected before posting off another piece.

A colleague of mine never has less than 25, I repeat, 25 MSS out at any one time. Those rejected she immediately re-writes and sends off to another editor. She sells most of her stuff abroad and it can take months and months before she gets a reply. She'd never know where she was if she didn't keep a strict record.

You won't, of course, be working so prodigiously – YET. But at the stage you've now reached in this book, you should be sending outlines to editors at the rate of at least one a week, if you're serious about becoming a journalist.

Don't expect the editor to reply by return of post to your outline. The average wait is perhaps a couple of months – some take longer.

Yet another function of records – they tell you where your MS has BEEN. It's the height of embarrassment and non-professionalism if you submit a piece to the same editor twice.

**RECORD OF SUBMISSIONS – (Left-hand Page)**

| TITLE | SUBMITTED TO |
|-------|--------------|
|       |              |

**RECORD OF SUBMISSIONS – (Right-hand Page)**

| DATES | | | | AMOUNT £p |
|-------|----------|----------|------|-----------|
| SENT | RETURNED | ACCEPTED | PAID |           |
|      |          |          |      |           |

# Expenses allowed by the tax man

A plus point is that you can claim certain expenses against tax. Keep a faithful record and RECEIPTS of them all. You'll need this for your Tax Return every April. The Inland Revenue will let you claim for:

Postage,

Stationery,

Office equipment (new and depreciation of old) plus servicing and maintenance,

Rent on the room you work in (which you call your office),

Business travel,

Research materials (reference books/periodicals, photocopies, library reserves).

# Chapter 19

# Vive la Petite Différence

- Women's market: 'Four Cs'
- Psychology of women
- Ideas with woman appeal
- Exercise 16
- Men's market: 'Three Cs' (or more)
- Exercise 17

---

'THERE'S the reader who wants to share her wonderful idea with the world. Then there's the professional, and you read every word thoroughly.'

NOELLE WALSH, Editor, *Good Housekeeping*

---

IN THIS CHAPTER we're going to look at two specific markets – the categories 'Women' and 'Men' – and what they read.

## Women's market

This is by far the UK's largest consumer category merely because of the demand. But MEN – DON'T SWITCH OFF: many male writers make a very nice living writing exclusively for the women's Press. It offers journalists the widest scope. And many women's magazines pay freelances as highly as national newspapers.

Surveys reveal that women buy more magazines than men. Women, it seems, are genuinely interested in what their sisters do, plus making the most of being women and all that entails.

Women are insatiable for the 'Four Cs' (clothes, cosmetics, cooking, children). Stay with me, men, you'll be surprised at what I'm about to say. These four subjects apply right across the board whatever the class, level of affluence, intellect or age group. OK, so some women opt not to have children. But not wanting one of your own doesn't preclude your interest in relatives', friends' and neighbours' kids. (I adore horses and will go out of my a way to look at, stroke or ride one. But I don't want one living in my first floor London flat!)

All 'Four Cs' are usually handled by staffers. They *don't give a great deal of scope for freelance writers*, unless you're a specialist in one of the areas.

Having said that, I don't include EVERYTHING to do with children, for instance. Staffers handle the everyday 'how to bring up little Johnny, what to feed him on and what to do when he's got spots'. The areas freelances *can* explore are social problems – child abuse, education, lack of crèches, disabled kids, single parent dads.

The 'Four Cs' pages are also an enormous help when determining your reader profile. The products advertised indicate age/affluence/social strata, eg cordon bleu or economy dishes.

I find it an enigma that some beginner writers get all superior over the women's Press, considering it somehow trivial. Think again. This attitude merely illustrates just how amateur they are – and that they haven't studied the market.

## Psychology of women

Many female and male journalists make a living writing exclusively for the women's market. This is mainly because of the vast variety of subjects it offers the writer. As I've already mentioned, the majority of today's women hold down a job and have interests outside the home. A London *Evening Standard* survey tells us that three out of four British wives hold down an outside job. This will rise to 80 per cent in the next three years. They have interests beyond the domestic boundaries of the home.

To determine the demand, think objectively of a woman's psychological make-up. They're carers, they're supporters, they're organisers – therefore they have an avid interest in national and local current issues – the 'people problems' of today.

The market research project I set you in Chapter 6 must have revealed that women's magazines covered Buddhism, the Olympics, shortage of blood donors, Black Power, gardens for the blind, unemployment, championship chess, sexual inadequacy, pensions, nuclear disarmament, skiing, AIDS, football hooliganism, the ozone layer, Prince Charles, Nelson Mandela, Channel Tunnel . . . WHAT AM I SAYING TO YOU?

Yes – 90 per cent of all the topics under the sun. And there's not one of those not read by men. In fact, you'd be amazed at the large number of men who read women's magazines and the women's pages of newspapers. Even if they sneak a look when their wife/mother/sister is out of the room.

## Specialist market research

Have another visit to that newsagent. Go with an open mind. Look at all the women's mags. Ignore the Four Cs and list the other topics covered. You could be in for a surprise.

## Finding ideas

A good many women's magazines, newsmags and women's pages of the national Press are avid for features in which *women play significant parts in the community*. Please note that down. They like to feature women *facing challenges and overcoming problems*. They want personal and second-hand experiences plus *practical advice*.

**Example topics:** running a shelter for battered wives; running a recently dead husband's lorry hire service; bringing up a hyperactive child while coping with an aged parent; taking a party of teenagers on holiday; devising an original programme for the town's annual twinning event; combining an unusual career or money-making hobby with motherhood; novel charity fund-raising schemes.

As I've mentioned before, some of the best pieces are spurred by indignation. Hasn't something happened to you or someone else which has infuriated you? Could be this is the second time a heavy lorry has parked on the pavement outside your home and smashed the paving stones? Walking is hazardous. Perhaps there's been a sprained ankle or a pushchair has overturned harming the baby. Your fury would come over well in words. So many readers would identify with you.

But remember, the piece is just an unsaleable whinge and is no more than a 'reader's letter', unless you give it balance by quoting other people's similar experiences (good and bad). Interview neighbours and lorry drivers – suggest solutions. Say what action you took (reported the incident to the local council?). You could have an emotive piece for a women's magazine, the local paper or a newsmagazine.

And I've read at least four pieces on the agonies of having the builders in. They're popular with editors.

Are the men still with me? They could write about lorries and builders too.

Exasperation comes over well if the words are tinged with satirical wit. Try and give your work some humour, even if you're poking the finger of ridicule at yourself.

You can find saleable ideas in the driest places. A colleague of mine happened to see an advert for a conference on dowsing (using a diviner's rod to find water and other elements). 'What an odd subject for a conference,' thought she. The ad gave a very brief run-down on what was on the agenda. On the list was dowsing for health. This stumped Catherine – what on earth was that about?

Her journalist's curiosity aroused, she sent for a prospectus. Sure enough, it said that dowsing can be used to help diagnose certain diseases. What an unusual angle.

So she sent an outline to the features editor of *Best* – were they interested? Yes, and so much so they gave her a commission. She got £200, plus an entrance fee for the conference, plus a fee for a personal analysis while she was there. Plus her fares.

So, keep an eye open for conferences and seminars. After all, the staff writers can't cover *every* interesting event.

The same author recently had a piece accepted on a haunted village. This focused on the effects the ghost had on inhabitants.

# Two other ideas sources

Look at upmarket glossies like *Over 21, Elle, Options, New Woman, Marie Claire, Good Housekeeping, Woman's Journal* and that ilk, plus the newsmags I mentioned in previous chapters. The sort of really deep issues that made saleable features were two I saw recently that any competent beginner could have handled: 'How to cope when your other half is a workaholic' and 'Why women stay loyal to violent men'. Both subjects affect thousands of women. That's their appeal. Many readers identify. For more subjects to write up, think of women objectively and their problems.

I would hazard a guess that the source of ideas for the authors of both those features was the AGONY COLUMNS.

Read through a few and you'll discover topics which you could expand and make into a feature. What you need are other people's similar experiences. Mention the subject you choose to every woman you can – friends, women at bus stops and in supermarket checkout queues. Among a dozen, you'll find perhaps ten who switch off, yes, but there will be two who have had the experience you're researching or know someone who has.

This is how to strike up a conversation with a stranger. You're in the doctor's or dentist's waiting room, in the supermarket checkout queue, or at the bus stop. You glance at your watch and turn to the woman next to you: 'I wish it/they/he would hurry up. I've got to go and see my neighbour. Her husband drinks heavily and she's lots of problems' (or whatever is the angle you want to write up). Chances are this will bring no response. But sometimes the woman will answer: 'Really? My sister's husband does too. She's always short of money, etc, etc.' And so you have a conversation going which will give you interesting anecdotes for your feature.

*Don't tell them you're a journalist.* Because of the crimes of the gutter press 'journalist' is now a four-letter word. All of us are tainted. The women will clam up on you. They fear they're going to be plastered all over a daily or Sunday tabloid.

Another ideas source is LETTERS TO THE EDITOR. You get a good inkling of the issues being talked about TODAY. Use the same method – talk to as many women as you can. Remember it's quotes that 'bring the language alive' and turn it into journalism.

By the way, you'll notice I didn't include in that upmarket mag list *Cosmopolitan* and *Company*. Neither takes unsolicited material.

## EXERCISE 16

Get an idea from either the Agony Columns or Letters to the Editor and write a feature for a women's magazine.

Don't let this be merely an academic exercise for this book. Concentrate on finding a genuine market and on identifying an idea that really will sell. Then promote it in an outline letter and send it to the features editor of the magazine you've chosen BEFORE you write it up.

# Men's market

The situation used to be that the only magazines men read were on sport, cars, gardening and sex. For journalists, they're all pretty exclusively male provinces, unlike the women's market which has male and female contributors.

In the last few years publishing has woken up to the fact that, macho image or not, thousands of men are interested in cooking (as many live alone), clothes and cosmetics (though they use the term 'toiletries' for aftershave, shaving creams, hair gel and deodorants). So that's 'Three Cs' for men and 'Four Cs' for women. (For males you can still include three other 'Cs' – cars, cricket and crumpet!) These pages in men's mags are just as helpful to determine a reader profile.

This isn't just a surmise. No publisher can afford to launch a magazine unless he gets encouraging results from professional market surveys. These always hinge on consumer products – what is the target readership interested in buying? The survey indicates which types of product manufacturers will be willing to take adverts. Magazines get the major part of their revenue from advertisers, not from the cover price.

So to name most of the new wave of men's mags, there's: *Sky*, which is sort of unisex but is predominantly male, *Arena*, *The Face*, *Gentleman's Quarterly*, *For Him* and *Ebony Man*. (By the way, this book is written in a recession and magazines can close at

any time. So check at your newsagent's to see if they still exist
rather than rely on me.)

*Arena* and *The Face* are aimed at male adolescents. They all take
profiles of celebrities (few consumer mags don't), the other topics
are the obvious ones, cars, sport, pin-ups, restaurants, reviews of
films, shows and videos. Some of them carry features on finance
especially for young 'would-be high achievers'.

I assessed editions of *GQ* which carried in-depth features: one
on Gary Lineker's legs(!), another on 'Gambling Around the
World', and a great one on 'How Women Turn Men On'.

*For Him* carried 'Why Crime DOES Pay', and a controversial
piece on abortion with quotes from men with pro and anti views.
Any aspiring journalist could have thought up that last topic, an
unusual one for a men's publication, and gone out and done the
interviews. What other unusual subjects could a men's magazine
be tempted to accept? How about single fathers' rights, Cohabi-
tation Contracts, women priests, rape? Try CIPP on all these.

And then: 'Real men are cultured, enjoy sports, women and
*Esquire*', says the blurb. The British version of *Esquire* was
launched in spring 1991. An import from the US, the editor says,
in an interview in *Journalist's Week: 'Esquire* puts into words what
men have only felt in a fairly inchoate way . . . it's an articulate
companion about the male experience.'

Said to be 'About men and what men think of women', *Esquire*
has a literary heritage in the States which includes such writers as
Steinbeck, Hemingway, Mailer and Wolfe. The editor's aim, he
says, is to 'liberate magazine journalism . . . we can perhaps give
writers ways of expressing themselves, give them challenges to
find a new form, to cultivate a voice that isn't quite yet found. And
in the end create a magazine of real journalistic distinctiveness.'
Why don't you give it a try? Find out the editor's name so you can
put it on the outline letter.

The girlie mags aren't all cheesecake. Well *Mayfair* and *Club
International* are (anyway, they don't accept freelance material).
But *Penthouse, Playboy* and *Men Only* allow that men occasionally
do have other thoughts apart from sex. They're in the market for
profiles on big, butch men doing big, butch things as well as macho
film and TV personalities. They also like humour plus pieces on
how to get rich – the power struggle.

Another unisex mag that has a strong bias towards men is *Excel*. Their reader demand is for profiles of high achievers.

In general, don't write up blatantly obvious ideas. It'll have been done before. Go for the esoteric angle.

## EXERCISE 17

Go and look at the men's titles in the newsagent's, then think up a genuine selling angle for the men's market. It can be a crop of interviews on an emotive subject like single parent dads, or a Day-in-the-Life-of piece, somebody like a bloke in the Crime Squad. First research your magazines, find out from the *Writer's Handbook* the number of words they use and write up a feature.

As with the previous exercise, make this a genuine effort to write a saleable piece and not a mere academic exercise. Send off an outline to the editor first. At this stage in the book you should be selling your work.

# Chapter 20

# More Writing Tips

- Anecdotes
- Humour
- Description
- Illustrations
- Exercise 18

- Photographs and photographers
- Phoning editors
- Waiting for answers
- Re-writes

---

'THE commercial writer retains artistic integrity, but competes in an arena where amateur is a dirty word.'

FREDDIE SADLER, comedy writer

---

HERE ARE yet more tips to help you hone your work into pieces an editor will recognise and respect as journalism. In general, news features, profiles and reviews all have similar basic tenets, whatever the readership. They apply to the women's and men's magazines dealt with in the last chapter, and every other market.

## Anecdotes

As with quotes, anecdotes give a feature human interest. Can you define anecdote? My dictionary tells me it's a short narrative of an incident in private life. I'd call it a personal experience. They are often used as examples of a point the author is making.

**Example:** I wrote a piece on Neighbourhood Caring. The theme was: 'How is it that old people can die in their beds and not be

160

discovered for weeks?' The answer: 'Many people just do not care'. I strengthened my argument by including a true personal anecdote. One winter night the rain was sleeting down, I was in bed with flu and a temperature of 100°, but had to go out as I was desperate to buy some aspirins. I fainted in the street. The first thing I saw when I came to was a man's legs as he stepped over me. He didn't stop.

On reading that you were probably incensed at his attitude. Giving an anecdote immediately makes an incident more 'personal'. The readers thinks: 'It happened to a real person,' and subconsciously they react emotionally.

Let me make your toes curl up by giving you another true anecdote which I used to illustrate the hazards of laziness.

I was the features editor in a newspaper office. The company wasn't famous for supplying equipment – in the minuscule kitchen next door there was one teaspoon for making tea. (It was tied to the tap with a piece of string!) In the main office, on the sub's table, there was a single pair of scissors.

The cub reporter's job was to make endless cups of tea for the rest of us. He'd put in sugar, but would never stir it. We all regularly trooped back to the kitchen to use THE SPOON.

One day Walter, the layout artist, came back to his desk looking decidedly green. He'd been in the men's loo, and was followed by Dave, the sub. Walter had heard the sound of 'snip, snip' coming from one of the cubicles. Dave had emerged clutching his scissors. He'd informed Walter with a grin that he always cut his toenails in the men's loo.

Languid Walter could never drum up enough energy to go to the kitchen to stir his tea with the spoon. The sub's table was next to his draftboard and he had always borrowed the scissors as a stirrer.

# Humour

As for humour, my Chambers dictionary has a lovely definition: 'a mental condition which apprehends and delights in the ludicrous and mirthful'. Everyone likes to laugh. If you can write good humour most editors will pay you nicely for it.

But it's difficult. All experienced authors agree that the two toughest subjects to write about are sex and humour. I can't tell you how to do it. It's something that's inherent in the writer. If it doesn't come naturally then you haven't got it. The so-called humour of beginner writers is all too often heavily laboured or unnecessarily malicious. Bad humour (unfunny or distasteful) can be a reason for rejection.

## Description

When you're giving a description, remember that all the reader has to rely on for an exact mental picture is your words.

Adjectives such as 'old', 'young', 'large', 'small', and the like don't have more than a very basic meaning.

**Example:** 'He was an old man.' Doesn't say a great deal, but: 'He was old enough to have fought in World War I,' makes a tremendous contribution to the reader's mental picture.

The same goes for large measurements. Suppose you're doing a profile of a successful, affluent actor and want to describe his house and garden. Something like 'it was xxx metres long' really doesn't mean much to any but the technically-minded. To get across size you need to compare it with something familiar.

**Example:** 'The garden was xxx metres long; you could get two tennis courts into it.'

**Example:** 'The medieval barn was xxx metres square. It could have accommodated four three-storey houses.'

## Illustrations

The editor can get an illustration for your feature, but if you supply it you get paid extra. It also gives work extra reader appeal. Illustrations could be photos, drawings, paintings or cartoons. But they have to be to a professional standard.

The most common are photos, but don't submit colour snaps. They wouldn't be accepted. This is a technical issue, not an editorial decision. It applies equally to black and white photos as well as colour, also to paintings in colour (not line drawings or cartoons).

Photos and paintings have to have sharp outlines to reproduce in print. Slightly out-of-focus prints reproduce even 'smudgier' than on the original (just don't bother to send them in, it stamps you as a rank amateur). Colour prints also smack of the green beginner.

## EXERCISE 18

As you know, newspapers mostly use black and white photos. But for the occasional colour picture, what do you think they want – prints, negatives or transparencies? Think hard before you look up the answer at the back of the book.

# Photographs and photographers

Few of us are competent photographers unless it's a hobby we've studied. But technology has advanced cameras so much it's not now so difficult to take clear photos.

If the publication uses ONLY black/white pix, it's important to put a black/white film in your camera in the first place. Only amateurs use a colour film and hope the publication's printers can make good black/white pictures from their prints. These are never particularly successful, and can be the reason the piece is rejected.

Alternatives are a professional Press photographer. Notice I said PRESS photographer. Wedding photographers are easiest to find as they have high street shops. But professionally they are at the bottom of the heap. They can usually take only static groups. A Press photographer works very fast with a hand-held camera in black/white or colour, whichever you state.

How do you find a Press photographer? Ring your local newspaper, ask for the Picture Desk. Speak to the photographer there and see if he or she'll do a job for you. This is general practice in the trade. They'll usually oblige, and hopefully won't charge too much.

Can you think of any other ways of finding a high quality photographer? Try the Yellow Pages.

A School of Photography is another good contact. Second or third year students can usually do a good job.

The local camera club is another source. This would be much cheaper. But of course, the members don't have the experience. And they, like photography students, may only be able to take portraits of stationary models using a camera on a tripod with lots of arty lighting. You probably don't need that type of photographer. if you want ACTION shots, that means a person expert with a hand-held camera who can work rapidly. The action only happens once, there's no second chance. If the photographer's experience is only of taking people who stand and pose, then they would most likely fail you.

## Briefing photographers

If you do engage a photographer, brief them thoroughly beforehand:

(1) describe the shot you want in detail,
(2) explain what you want the shot to achieve.

Just like a writer, a photographer is a creative person, so discuss exactly what you want the finished picture to do – bring out the vast size of the subject, or its smallness, or the scruffiness of the area or whatever. A creative photographer will have effective suggestions of their own.

Then shut up. *How* they take the photo is not your province. They're in charge of the camera and would rightly resent it if you tried to tell them how to take the picture.

## Free prints

You don't always have to supply your own photos. If you're writing pieces on subjects like history or archaeology, then museums will supply you with prints – often gratis. Photos are also free from tourist offices. Another source very generous with free photos is show business and publishing.

# Taking your own

Let's say you're up against a very tight deadline. The editor wants the written piece plus black/white pix on his desk tomorrow. You may have to take the photos yourself. See what I said in Chapter 11 about prints, transparencies, sizes and getting film developed fast.

# Keep your originals

By the way, if you take your own photos, never, NEVER, under any circumstances part with either the negative or the original transparency, not even for money. If it's a good picture you can possibly sell it several times over – first with the feature, then to a number of editors as just a picture/caption. All the editor buys is what you send, a PRINT, not the negative, or a DUPLICATE TRANSPARENCY, not the original.

# Phoning Editors

If you're writing a news story or an ultra-topical news feature, there's no time to post an outline and wait for the reply. You'll have to phone for a quick editorial decision. Before you dial an editor, write yourself a script. Note on the left side of a piece of A4 paper all the questions you want to ask, leaving space on the right to write down their answers. Also at the top of the page put the date, phone number and person to whom you spoke with their name spelled correctly (ask them) and their title.

This method gives you three advantages:

1   It ensures you ask all the questions you want to. When actually on the phone to an editor you'll naturally be a trifle nervous, and vital questions could go out of your head.

2   It saves everyone's time when you have a straightforward, logical conversation without any 'ums' and 'ers'. It gives the editor an impression of a good professional.

**3** You have a record of what you said and what he said. Your questions should include: 'What specific points do you want me to cover?', 'How many words do you want?' 'What's the deadline?', 'Are you giving me a commission?'

And if he says 'yes', this is the time to discuss money. It's up to you to get the best price. If your story is good enough for them to offer you a commission, then they're keen. You've thought up something unique. So, when you ask how much he'll give, hesitate a couple of seconds after his reply; then ask for more. Explain the vast amount of work you've already put into research/interviewing before you can even start writing.

Don't be your average British wimp who turns pale and speechless at the mere thought of negotiating a price. Immediately after you're offered the commission is your brief, propitious moment of strength. So this is when you say: 'How much are you offering?' and then: 'Sorry, I can't do it for that. I need at least £xxx.' The editor will often agree the larger amount.

And don't forget – whatever fee you finally agree on, you then say: 'Plus expenses.' And be fair here. Get receipts, keep rail and plane tickets, get an itemised telephone bill (British Telecom will give you a preliminary one). The editor can't refuse if you can *prove* the expenses you've incurred in writing the story.

All this, of course, is only if he says: 'Yes' when you ask: 'Are you offering me a commission?'

By the way, a commission is legally binding even if it's only verbal. And as the editor will never (or seldom) confirm it in writing, don't forget to bang off a letter immediately you put down the phone:

Dear (editor's name)

This is to confirm our telephone conversation this afternoon when you commissioned me to write a 1,500 word exposé on corruption in the local council and agreed to pay me £300, plus expenses. I will deliver on or before your deadline, Tuesday, 22 May.

# How long should I wait?

As for the less topical pieces – looking for a reply to the outline or finished feature you sent on spec you sometimes have to wait months – and months.

There are all sorts of reasons:

- They're sitting on it till they're let down by a writer they've commissioned and they need a stopgap;
- They're planning a multi-feature on the subject next year;
- The editor's busy;
- The editor sort of likes it and sort of doesn't – he's thinking about it;
- The inefficient Post Office didn't deliver it;
- The envelope was so illegibly addressed they couldn't deliver it;
- It fell on the floor so the office cleaner threw it away;
- It was so badly presented/written it was 'binned' in disgust;
- The editor liked it, put it in a 'special' pile, and it got swamped by other papers put on top of it;
- You forgot to include your name/address/phone number;
- The editorial assistant uses it to stand the kettle on;
- The reader is on maternity leave . . .

Do you want me to go on? I could – ad nauseam.

After six to eight weeks always write or phone to ask if it's going to be accepted. If after repeated letters/phone calls the response is negative, BE PHILOSOPHICAL – and POSITIVE. Wave it goodbye. Treat the situation as though you've never submitted the piece. Send it off to a different market.

If your copy is topical you wouldn't wait, of course. You can't afford to as the piece has a 'sell by' date. Always in the outline put something along the lines of: 'As this is topical I need to have your reply within three days, please. I'll ring you on Wednesday for your decision.'

# Re-writes

When the editor rings you and says: 'I loved your piece, but . . .' – don't throw a wobbly.

The need for a re-write doesn't signal the end of your career.

And you've the editor's objective criticism to help you. Be
POSITIVE.

Perhaps your piece contains comments that could stretch the
credibility of the magazine, or possibly land a libel suit. Or you
could have strayed off the point, or you're metaphorically
trampling on the publication's stated policy.

Requests to re-work a few sentences are taken on the chin by the
professional. It's only amateurs and prima donnas who shout
'shan't'. A certain amount of re-writing is a pretty regular editorial
call (ultimatum, in fact). So, rather than be surprised (and affron-
ted), expect it.

If the editor is merely being bloody-minded, don't call her rude
names. Merely withdrew the piece and try it somewhere else.

# Chapter 21

# More Ideas

- Silly Season
- Exercises 19 and 20
- MPs' speeches
- Exercise 21
- Facts – your responsibility
- Fillers
- Problems: fear of failure, coping with rejection

---

'REJECTION is part of any creative art. Think of Hemingway, he was rejected hundreds of times. I immediately get back to the keyboard and work harder.'

CORK MILLNER, Journalist (USA)

---

HERE ARE yet more saleable ideas for you.

## Silly Season

National newspapers need features for the 'Silly Season'.

### EXERCISE 19

When is the Silly Season? – What is it? – What causes it? (think – before looking up the answers at the back of the book).

In the Silly Season you will have noticed a rash of Loch Ness Monster pieces. The national Press resurrects all the old chestnuts. It's an ideal opportunity for freelances with an original idea. This is a good time for anniversary pieces – it's XX number of months/years since Marilyn Monroe died or the *Titanic* sank or Terry Waite was freed. Those are national issues, and they need to be to interest the major editors, but they will put their own writers on those. Dig out something esoteric. Don't go for the obvious.

Forward-thinking journalists will have been on the lookout last year for big news. They keep the clips in their cuttings files and around about May or June they investigate the current situation, the REPERCUSSIONS of that event.

**Example:** There was a severe village flooding. Your follow-up feature asks and answers questions such as: 'What did the locals do about it', 'What's the position today?', 'Can it ever happen again?' And there you have a TOPICAL feature. Remember what I said about newspaper editors hailing topicality as their god.

**Example:** Another follow-up piece: you read last year that a teaching hospital started a 12 month project to survey – what? – perhaps the effect on families of having a teenager with AIDS. Discover how the project is going. What are their findings? When will results be published? Will they be published at all? If so, what action will be taken?

**Example:** Joe Bloggs, who set up the British/World record for XX this time last year, is now . . .

Always keep an eye open for news items you can follow up.

Don't bother with topics like the Queen Mum's birthday or the Notting Hill Carnival. They'll be covered by staff reporters who have time on their hands because Parliament is in recess.

## EXERCISE 20

Write a national newspaper feature for the Silly Season. First research and decide on which paper it's for. Then, either send it off if you're reading this in the summer, or file it until next June, then send in an outline.

# MPs' speeches

Let's look more closely at your cuttings files. The Silly Season isn't the only time you can use them. If you have up-to-date clips on an unusual subject, any time there's a biggish news report on that topic you can offer an editor a NEWS FEATURE to be printed next day.

I say an unusual topic, because all the obvious ones will be written up by staff reporters. The big attraction for the editor will be that your piece is TOPICAL, ie about something that's in the news now.

**Example:** A top-ranking MP speaks in the House on litter in the streets. You know the entire Press will report it because it's an established thorn in the side of this particular MP and he'll have some pretty heavy comments to make.

What you do is ring your local daily paper, tell them that Bloggs MP is speaking on Litter in the Streets next Tuesday, and would they be interested in a short feature on the filthy streets in your particular part of town?

The streets are so neglected, there are even masses of weeds growing. Some of them are two feet high – urban streets starting to look rural. Some weeds have nasty effects if parts are eaten by children (such as deadly nightshade or laburnum). What other risks? The feature isn't particularly riveting, but the mere fact that it's linked with the newspaper's coverage of what Bloggs said in the House makes it highly saleable.

All that would be necessary on your part is a regular scan through the published speakers' questions in the House, a cuttings file marked POISONOUS BRITISH PLANTS, a wander round your own streets (you need spot only one poisonous weed) – and you're in business. The rest is your journalistic creativity.

This is a hypothetical example. But this summer two-foot-tall weeds *were* growing in my street, so I'm not giving you an impossible topic.

Now don't ask me how you find out in advance what's on the House of Commons agenda – that's part of research. Where would you go for starters?

The Public Reference Library. I'll give you one clue only, Tabled Questions are published by HMSO.

## EXERCISE 21

Get hold of the Tabled Questions and find a topic which you could follow up with a feature.

# Facts – your responsibility

Just a reminder – DOUBLE-CHECK YOUR FACTS, like name spellings, dates, venues. It's the author's responsibility to get the facts right, not the editor's. Should they print your piece and a reader tells them something's incorrect, that publication will never use you again. You've shown you're unreliable.

# Fillers

What are they? Very brief pieces popular with magazines to fill up the page when the main piece falls short of the bottom of the page. Some mags like *Take A Break*, *Best*, *Bella*, *Me* and *Chat* devote whole pages to them.

*Reader's Digest* is great for fillers. And the pay is excellent. They have four spots: *Life's like that*, *Humour in Uniform*, *Laughter is the Best Medicine* and anecdotes at the end of each full-length feature. One tip about *Reader's Digest*, don't send them longer freelance material. It's all commissioned or syndicated.

# Problems

Are you submitting work to editors?

I'm actually working with you blind. I can't know whether or not you do the exercises or are sending out work.

I'm NOT about to read you the Riot Act. At the beginning of this book I warned you journalism was a tough subject. My concern is whether or not I'm failing you. If you're not getting work published, is it because I've not given you enough guidance or because you've not taken it in and acted on it?

So my thought process is this. Your motivation to buy this book must have been that you had something to say to others. My job is to take your inherent writing talent and help you shape it into a style that will be accepted by editors.

What I can't do is write or submit pieces to editors for you.

I appreciate that few beginner journalists are prepared for perhaps the biggest half of getting their work printed – the MARKETING. It's an enormous hurdle to overcome. But this path has been trodden by thousands of would-be journalists before you, INCLUDING ME. And I *know* it's scary.

I remember the same inhibition about sending work to editors. Hell, I still have it. I don't think you ever become completely blasé about it. But if I sit down and analyse it, I have to admit that the fear is not of the editor, but of REJECTION.

I've created a piece. I've done my best, it's my baby. Like any mother I'm fiercely protective.

Why am I afraid of rejection? Because, indirectly, the editor is rejecting *me* . . . It's quite deeply psychological.

This crisis of confidence is a normal stage in all learning processes.

Which of you didn't lack confidence at school? – at college? – going for job interviews? You've trodden this path before, haven't you?

Let me give you a thought to pin on the wall above your typewriter: THE ULTIMATE FAILURE IS TO MIND SO MUCH ABOUT REJECTION THAT YOU STOP TRYING.

Please read the above with application as it affects EVERY writer and is perhaps the toughest problem to cope with because it touches our very psyche.

Accept that YOU WILL GET REJECTION SLIPS. It's a fact of journalistic life. You can't win them all.

And when your work arrives back in its stamped addressed envelope, it thuds through the letterbox on to the mat – and your heart thuds down into your soul and your soles. You *can't* approach it the same way as you would if there wasn't any Camembert cheese at Sainsburys today, so never mind, you'll have Brie instead. This is psychological disappointment.

But if you let it develop into a sackcloth and ashes situation – and worse, a depression perhaps – you're severely sabotaging your chances of getting into print. OK, beat your breast, howl, shed a few tears and kick hell out of the kitchen sink. Then sit down and

ANALYSE. What thinking people do is turn rejection on its head. Look at it POSITIVELY. My piece was returned – WHY? If it was what the editor WANTED it wouldn't have been sent back.

Turn back to my *Checkpoints* on page 83. Was it right for the market? Was it the right length? Did I have a genuinely interesting angle? Did I give readers something NEW about that angle? Was what I said worth reading about? And all the other points.

If you can *truly* answer 'yes' to all the Checkpoint questions, then your piece is of professional standard. So the reason for rejection is one of non-suitability, *not* of being sub-standard.

So YOU HAVE NOT FAILED. Failing is not doing well enough, not being up to standard. But even if your piece *is* up to standard this doesn't guarantee its acceptance. The great intangible is the editor's personal criterion. It's the demand she has in her head at that moment. She's planning an edition, she has this, this and this, she now needs *that*. For metaphorical simplicity – she has for her fruit salad bananas, grapes, peaches and apples. She now needs oranges. You send her apples. They could be the best standard apples in England, but they're not what she wants. So she returns your piece. YOU HAVEN'T BEEN REJECTED. It's merely that your piece was unsuitable at that particular time. Sent, say, a year later, it could well be that the same editor will accept it joyfully.

# Chapter 22

# How to Review

- Books, films, shows
- Getting started
- House style
- Other ways in
- Writing tips
- 'Bad' crits

- Trade Press
- Payment
- Exercise 22
- Stan Nicholls reviews fantasy books

'*The Observer* and *Sunday Times* still review books that 99 per cent of people don't give a toss for. Until this generation of reviewers dies out, or is preferably shot, we're not going to get anywhere. They still think it's 1950 and Evelyn Waugh is the best writer in England.'

JOHN JARROLD, Director, Orbit/Macdonald Publishers

AH, REVIEWING – one of these areas where you *can* express opinions. And all those lovely free books and tickets for films and shows. Great. It's one of the hats I wear. One year I went to every Christmas show in London. There were 26 of them! I'm going to call again on our tame journalist, Stan Nicholls, to give you some tips on this. He's reviewed thousands of books, films, plays and videos.

But before I interview him for you, let's look at this cornucopia of freebies with a critical eye.

You're never going to pay the rent with reviewing. It's not a very cost-effective project. To the time it takes to write the review you still have to add the hours spent watching the play or reading the book. It doesn't work out at a very lucrative rate per hour.

Even the NUJ advocate low rates for reviewing. It's best to look upon reviewing as an adjunct to writing features and other stuff.

OK, so you go to the cinema and read books anyway. But editors don't always want reviews of the films and books you want to see.

True reviewing isn't merely spouting your opinions. It's being informative, entertaining in style and assessing the work for the publication's readership.

**Example:** There's a new book on erotic Indian carvings and you're dying to review it. But the obvious markets, *Penthouse* etc, and upmarket women's mags, will probably have been sent a copy direct. So for them reviewing will be a staff job. For other mags the subject may be taboo. Or it's merely out of the sphere of their readers' interest: eg for *Motor Cycle News* or *Computer Weekly*. So you'd have problems persuading the publishers to send you a copy of the book.

If you don't live near London, film previews could be a problem as they're usually held in the West End at 10 a.m. And no, you can't take a friend. To be invited it helps if you first get a commitment from an editor that the review will be printed.

As for plays – how do you make notes in the dark?

If you get serious about reviewing and are REGULARLY in print, there's an association to join. The Critics' Circle (established 1913) promotes the art and upholds its integrity. 47 Bermondsey St, London SE1 3XT. Tel: 071–403 1818.

Because of its popularity, reviewing is a very competitive field. Everyone wants to be in there. But it is possible for beginner journalists to force the door open if they have enough stamina and tenacity. One of the keys to unlock that door is a thorough study of the market.

Let's now ask Stan Nicholls a few questions.

# Getting started

*Joan:* How does a beginner break into reviewing?

*Stan:* Market research cannot be emphasised too strongly. Study half a dozen issues of the magazine or newspaper you want to review for. Then, in the case of books, buy three or four and review them yourself.

Try to write them in the house style of the market you're aiming for. Send them to the review editor or features editor, explain that you don't expect them to print the reviews, you're enclosing them merely as an example of what you're capable of.

It might not be a bad idea, before you go to the expense of buying the books, to ring the editor first and ask if you can do this. On the understanding that you don't expect to be either published or paid for this work, it can be a GOOD INVESTMENT. I've done this on occasion. Once you've proved you can do it, they're more likely to give you commissions, and send you the book or tickets for the play/film.

# Style – does it matter?

*Joan:* What about the style?

*Stan:* HOUSE STYLE is extremely important. Each publication has its own distinctive style of language. Therefore, a review for *The Times* is not the same as for the *Daily Mirror*. It's self-evident: but beginner writers forget that. Editors tell me all the time that the main weakness in the pieces they receive is the execution of the material. It isn't the content. It's quite simply that it's been sent to the wrong publication. In other words, the writer didn't do the market research.

Study the market – study the house style – try to hit their beat. Every successful publication has its own 'voice'. (At the end of this chapter I've include one of the review columns Stan writes for *The Dark Side* so you can see the publication's 'voice'.)

# Other ways in

*Joan:* What other ways are there of getting into the field?
*Stan:* Sometimes I'll come across a novel which I think shows considerable promise. Perhaps it had a few good reviews but not much coverage. (Most books sink without trace – 62,000 titles were published in the UK in 1990, of which half were new fiction. They can't *all* be reviewed in *The Times*, *Observer*, *Financial Times* or *Independent*.)

If you contact publishers courteously and can convince them you're a genuine reviewer and not just trying to get free books, you can get yourself put on their mailing lists and get advance notice of the books to be published.

When you've had a few reviews printed you then have an 'in'. And they don't necessarily need to be favourable ones as publishers are very much into the idea that *any* coverage is good coverage.

When you've established yourself as a published journalist you can ask publishers to put you on the list for advance copies of books permanently.

Every couple of months they send out a list of authors they'll have available for interviews. All publishers do that. All you need do is explain your special areas of interest.

# Writing tips

*Joan:* What tips can you give on the actual writing?
*Stan:* The way you approach the writing is also determined by the market. If you look at the *New York Review of Books*, for example, you might find 10,000-word reviews; really in-depth ones. Then look at some UK women's magazines and you'll often find 50-word reviews. This is an art. It takes a lot of skill to write with such brevity. So the market dictates the way in which you write the review.

In the case of a novel, you might compare it with previous novels written by the same author. That's always a good thing to do. You might compare the book with works by other authors who could have been an influence, or who write in the same genre.

With a first novel you could always say: 'This writer is out of the tradition of Hemingway,' – or whoever.

It's always a good idea to include a BRIEF SYNOPSIS. But don't give away the end of the book or film. That's very unfair and you'd be extremely unpopular. It's also very unprofessional.

## 'Bad' crits

*Joan:* Now, what about adverse criticism?

*Stan:* You have to play them as you see them. You're not being paid to be wishy-washy – 'Well, I quite liked that' – just because you got a freebie. Forget all that. You're being paid for your objective opinion, and naturally sometimes that opinion is going to be unfavourable. The important thing is to say positively that you like it, and why; or that you don't like it, and why.

Cite reasons – summon your evidence and lay it out. Journalism, like any other kind of writing, should be entertaining. Too many reviews are rather turgid. They run through the contents, and sum up: 'Well it was quite good, not as good as his last film, but probably better than his next one.' Readers don't want that. It's the old adage that BAD NEWS IS GOOD NEWS.

Editors like controversial, contentious, acid-dipped reviews. We all remember a good 'bad' review better than we remember a good 'good' review. So, if you can put the knife in – BUT FAIRLY – then you're more likely to sell the review. This may be a sad reflection on human nature, but nevertheless it's the way of the world.

The message to be underlined here is don't be afraid to express your views – good or bad – very POSITIVELY AND STRONGLY. Most people who are in the glitzy leisure-business machine (books, films, shows, videos) go through reviews with a ruler and measure the column inches. That's all they're interested in. The psychology is that if a name is mentioned often enough that's good. It almost doesn't matter what's said about them. That sounds cynical, but it happens to be true.

# Trade Press

*Joan:* What other tips do you have on breaking into the field?

*Stan:* Keep an eye on your Trade Press for news of publication launches in the pipeline. Write offering to review for them, sending samples of what you've had printed as your *bona fide*.

All new publications are on the lookout for talent to build up a stable of regular freelances, including reviewers. Get in on the ground floor.

Before the first edition hits the newsagents, send them a couple of really tasty ideas, angled at what you surmise their readership will be (suggested by the title). Include photocopies of your best printed reviews.

Then, don't wait for them to contact you. Give a few days for the post to arrive and the features editor to read your stuff, then phone them and ask: 'Have you had an opportunity to read my outline(s)? Can you use it/them?'

# Getting paid

*Joan:* What can you do if editors take ages to pay?

*Stan:* Not a lot. Writers are little people. OK, you've got the NUJ, the Institute of Journalists and others, but basically, freelances tend to be individuals, and can't bring any effective collective pressure. And there's a lot of us fish in the ocean.

Funnily enough, I spent half of yesterday chasing up accounts. In the past I've been ripped off. I've not been paid; I've had work stolen and published under another name. But the worst examples have not been in this country.

I had a commission from an American magazine, sent in the review and never heard from them. I chased them for two years but just couldn't get a reply. So I gave up. Walking down the Charing Cross Road one day I picked up a copy of the magazine – and there was my piece under another name. What do you do? It's always tempting to tell the horror stories: but they're very, very rare.

*Joan:* The squeaky wheel gets oiled: on that premise does nagging for money help?

*Stan:* You can try. I do. Ring the magazine's Accounts Department every day. It does pay off sometimes.

Another point to make is that when a publisher goes out of business, let's say they go into liquidation, freelance contributors are not preferential creditors. This means that any monies left after liquidation of the assets goes to others like the Inland Revenue, Customs and Excise, the banks and the DSS. As usual, the poor old writer comes bottom of the pile. So those who can afford to absorb the loss don't have to, and those of us who have no choice have to lump it. When a company you have worked for as a journalist goes out of business the least you can usually hope for is a fraction of the fee you expected to get.

## EXERCISE 22

Write a review of a book, film, play, concert, show or video of your choice – maximum 200 words. But first, research the market and decide on a specific magazine or newspaper, so you can write in their house style.

On the following page is an example of a review column Stan has written for *The Dark Side*.

# FANTASY
# BOOKSHELF

> Lo it was written that
> Stan Nicholls would
> venture forth and read
> lots of big books with
> wizards and elves in
> them . . .

Fantasy and SF are traditional parking lots for writers not easily hammered into other categories. The argument is that some of our quirkiest and most eccentric talents might not have published outside these pigeonholes. No JRR Tolkien, Mervyn Peake, JG Ballard? Maybe.

Doubtless the claim is exaggerated. But offbeat authors, denied the mainstream, do find refuge in the *genre*. And while recession forces cutbacks to midlists, where new writers have their best chance of emerging – and publishers impose stricter categorisation – the worry is what happens when indefinable wackos like Howard Waldrop come along.

Fortunately, Waldrop was under the fence long before publishing's present difficulties. He has written several novels, but his reputation as a unique voice in speculative fiction rests on his short stories, nineteen of which appear in *Strange Things in Close Up* (Legend, £4.50). The book welds together two American collections from the late 80s, *All About Strange Monsters of the Recent Past* and *Howard Who?* Given the anomalous nature of his work, "Howard what?" could be a more pertinent question.

In 'The Ugly Chickens' an ornithologist learns that dodos did not become extinct in the 18th century; a flock survived in Northern Mississippi until the 1920s. He uncovers their real fate, which proves ironically banal. 'Ike at the Mike' is a parallel world story – a Waldrop speciality – set in a late 60s America where Kennedy is still president. Senator Elvis Presley and British ambassador William Pratt, better known in our continuum as Boris Karloff, are alarmed by the prospect of impending revolution. They take their minds off politics by enjoying the music of top jazz combo Dwight Eisenhower, the coolest clarinet player to come out of Kansas, and drummer Wild George S ('Shitkicker') Patton. Casting these worthies in such wildly inappropriate roles is somehow much more effective than any amount of head-on satire. Like watching Count Dracula using a bidet.

An obsession with B-movies is a running theme. 'Dr Hudson's Secret Gorilla' is part *homage*, part send-up, of terrible old schlock horror pics which invariably starred George Zucco. 'All About Strange Monsters of the Recent Past, has the world devastated by hordes of creatures from 50s films. Giant lizards, black scorpions and over-sized octopuses vie with Martian fighting machines, dinosaurs and deranged robots in reducing civilisation to rubble. Japan, with a bigger monster movie output, really gets it in the neck. A variation on the 'Monsters from the Id' idea in *Forbidden Planet*, the story has more sf movie references per sentence than any other I've read. As all are unnamed, pedants can have a ball identifying them.

Waldrop is playing with cultural metaphors, alternate histories, absurdity, and anything else he can think of to create a very entertaining hybrid form. I haven't a clue how to label this stuff – 'slipstream' would probably be the currently fashionable term – but neither does the author, as he cheerfully admits. Certainly he doesn't think of it as fantasy, having written only one piece readily identifiable as such, and says he dislikes the *genre*. Perhaps he'll hate being reviewed in a column like this. Too bad, Howard.

Equally classy, but about as far as you can get from all this zaniness, is Judith Merkle Riley's *In Pursuit of the Green Lion* (NEL, £15.99 hb; £9.99 trade pb), although it does share a similar brand of irreverent and idiosyncratic wit.

## THE WEEPING LADY

The novel is a sequel to *A Vision of Light*, which introduced heroine Margaret Kendall, a woman whose sense of independence sits uneasily in male-dominated 14th century England. The new book tells how Margaret, recently widowed, is dragged away from London to the country pile of aging ratbag Sir Hubert de Villiers and forced into marriage with his youngest son, defrocked monk Gregory. A bit weird – he scourges himself in fits of religious frenzy and writes lousy poetry – he is at least preferable to scheming older brother Sir Hugo. Despite herself, Margaret begins to fall for him.

Complications arise when the ghost of her ex-husband arrives to stick his oar in. But he's a breeze compared to the de Villiers' resident phantom, the Weeping Lady, a nagging shade who turns out to be Margaret's new mother-in-law. Then Gregory apparently dies in a war with the French. Margaret escapes her in-laws, followed by the ghosts, and discovers Gregory is actually being held prisoner by Count de Merard, a satanist who kills babies in order to increase his magical powers. Aided by friends Mother Hilde and alchemist Malachi, she mounts a rescue, with the Weeping Lady in hot pursuit. A bizarre quest, complicated by Malachi's attempts to conjure up the legendary Green Lion, which can transmute base elements into gold, ensues.

Riley, an academic by profession, has a pleasing, straightforward style. *Green Lion* does not patronise, moves at a fair clip and, in Margaret of Ashbury, presents a formidable and fetching protagonist. The epoch reads authentically, probably as a result of thorough research, and the magic looks convincing. Above all the novel avoids the Hollywoodish 'Merrie England' approach often to be found when Americans tackle our medieval past.

The temptation to push on and make a trilogy of Margaret's adventures is probably strong. There are hints. Which would be fine if a third book is of the same quality, but an open-ended series could stretch things a little too far.

# Chapter 23

# Radio

- National
- Features
- News and current affairs
- Magazine programmes
- Exercise 23
- Arts
- Religious affairs
- Education
- Going on air
- Regions
- Round the clock
- What they want
- Local involvement
- Read it aloud
- Training

'TURNING print journalists into radio hacks is not just a case of picking up a tape recorder. The reporting skills are the same, but the presentation is different. And the interviewing needs special techniques.'

HEATHER PURDY, Course Leader,
Leicester Sound Training Unit

RADIO JOURNALISM can become a magnificent obsession. Not only do you get to write the words – you might get to read them over the air. And interviewing can be particular fun when a local radio station lends you its recording equipment.

Prick up your ears for the next bit – RADIO USES A MUCH GREATER VOLUME AND VARIETY OF JOURNALISTIC NEWS AND COMMENT THAN THE ENTIRE NATIONAL PRESS. I bet that surprised you. It certainly did me when I heard it from the BBC.

For anyone wishing to become a radio journalist, the best advice I can give is LISTEN. Radio doesn't exist for those who merely have the vague idea that they'd like to give a talk on a favourite subject, or have their bit of gossipy news read out.

Radio is a distinctive communication method with its own possibilities, limitations and techniques. So LISTEN to what's broadcast.

It's no different from getting work published in newspapers, newsmags and magazines. You must STUDY THE MARKET.

Whatever idea you have, as a piece for radio you must tailor it for the medium. Ask yourself what station is most likely to use material of this sort? Is there a particular series on that particular station where it might fit? Have they used similar (but not *too* similar) items before? What *length* do they need?

Radio is far, far easier to break into than television. TV is more or less a closed shop. Acceptance of work by freelance journalists is so rare, it's almost non-existent. Unless you have a sister-in-law who's a TV producer, forget it altogether. It's a great medium for drama and situation comedies, but that's not what this book is about. So I'm concentrating on radio.

Let's look at the market potential.

# National radio

BBC's national network has Radios 1, 2, 3, 4 and 5. As you will guess, there are fewer opportunities for journalists on 1, 2 and 3 as they are mostly music. But Radio 4 is mainly the spoken word and just eats up current affairs pieces from staffers and freelances.

Just think of the huge amount of short topical pieces used by Radio 4's *Woman's Hour*.

Radio 5 is for writers who can handle children's entertainment, sport and adult education. These are further freelance opportunities, albeit limited ones.

And, as you know, a half-hour programme is only another word for feature.

Additionally, don't forget the British Forces Network and the World Service. Radio really is an enormous market.

By the way, the BBC doesn't take only news and other non-fiction items like short talks and documentaries. They're also interested in short fiction, 12 minutes long, for *Morning Story*.

**TABOOS** A word here about BBC taboos. You won't have your piece accepted if it contains brand name advertising, political bias, libel, excessive violence or (ambiguous, this one) 'bad taste'.

# Features

A feature can be just under 15 minutes long, or, more usually, just under half an hour. It can be on more or less any INTERESTING subject.

Initial ideas for features should be submitted in a brief outline to the Head of Talks & Documentaries, Broadcasting House, Portland Place, London W1A 1AA.

If it's accepted the author will be asked to expand it into a full *synopsis* plus writing two or three pages of script. Don't let the word synopsis frighten you: what they need is merely an outline with a lot of detail.

# News and current affairs

The slots open to freelances for news and current affairs are mainly on local radio. Why is this? Material for national programmes like *Today*, *The World at One*, *PM* etc is all commissioned or submitted by professional news agencies.

# Magazine programmes

If you have my scientific or medical knowledge, Radio 4's *Science Now* and *Medicine Now* are for you; but they aren't all weighty subjects. They recently broadcast a thought-provoking piece about a women returners scheme. There are many qualified women scientists who left work to raise a family and subsequently want to return to the laboratory bench. This shows that *Science Now* is interested in related human problems.

Daily slots like *Woman's Hour* and *You and Yours* use a limited amount of freelance material. If you're out working, why not ask a friend to record the programmes for you to analyse?

By the way, *Woman's Hour*, *You and Yours* and *Feedback* use listener's letters, BUT THEY'RE UNPAID. Nor is payment made to people who phone in to programmes like *Call Nick Ross*. Anyway, letters aren't journalism.

Two good Radio 4 spots for freelances are *In Touch* and *Does He Take Sugar*.

*In Touch* is a 30-minute weekly programme for visually handicapped people. As with all the programmes I'm mentioning, LISTEN to it regularly if you want to contribute. It does take some interesting stuff, all within the scope of newcomer journalists. Not only would you be earning money, you'd be helping people for whom TV, cinema and theatre are virtually useless because they are partially or totally blind.

*Does He Take Sugar* is a 30-minute weekly for people with any disability. Writers should not send complete scripts but a *treatment*. This again is similar to an outline. It states the idea plus how it would be developed as a talk.

There's far more scope for freelance magazine programmes on the regional stations (see later in this chapter).

## EXERCISE 23

Think up as many angles as you can to submit for *In Touch* and *Does He Take Sugar*. When you've made your list, work out some more by using the CIPP method. When you've compiled your extended list, see the suggestions I have at the back of the book in Answer 23.

# Arts

*Kaleidoscope* is broadcast twice on weekdays. It is open to ideas from freelancers suggesting contributions from people such as authors, artists, actors, composers, musicians, film/play directors and critics who are then invited on to the programme. Keep an eye open for talented, up and coming creative people. They will consider interviews on tape of between three and seven minutes, but length varies – and so do fees.

# Religious affairs

Religion may or may not be your forte, but you don't have to be a vicar to be able to submit pieces. The BBC use a huge amount of unsolicited material in *Pause for Thought, Thought for the Day, Prayer for the Day* and *Seeds of Faith*.

Particularly attractive is *Pause for Thought*, which is popular in style and personal in content. Submissions can be either the finished script or a synopsis. They also welcome freelances' suggestions for single documentaries; these should be addressed to Broadcasting House, Portland Place, London W1A 1AA.

# Education

Let's look at the three main headings – we'll get the negative ones out of the way first.

(1) *Open University:* only limited opportunities for outsiders as contributors have to be university teachers or similarly qualified specialists.

(2) *Continuing Education:* the BBC say: 'there's virtually no opportunity to accommodate unsolicited scripts. However, the Head of Continuing Education, Radio, welcomes SUGGESTIONS for future programmes.'

(3) *Schools:* They take quite a lot of stuff from freelances. The main difference between this and general broadcasting is that Schools series are planned *at least 18 months before transmission*.

The audience is clearly defined by age and sometimes by ability, so the writer needs a sympathy for a particular age group or ability range.

The BBC say:

Schools radio is equal in status to all other BBC departments. It is *not* a training ground from which writers then graduate to writing for adults. Contributors must have the additional discipline of writing to a close brief, of simplifying ideas and arguments, plus an ability to use vocabulary suitable for a child audience.

Listen to as many Schools programmes as possible. Study the published list of *Annual Programmes* available, free, each year from April onwards.

The contributor must be able to accept constant guidance from the producer, with whom the idea needs considerable discussion before being written.

There's scope for freelances who conduct interviews and write linking material for documentaries. Experience in using a tape recorder and editing tape are a distinct advantage.

## Going on air

One of the exciting factors about talks (features) for radio is that you will probably be invited to read them yourself. The shy ones certainly don't *have* to, but the braver ones will find this an added incentive.

From the freelance's viewpoint great things are in prospect due to the series of Parliamentary Acts, passed recently, aimed at reforming broadcasting. Scheduled for 1992 are two new national commercial stations. Remember I said previously that a journalist is a small business? Well, the Government has decreed that a percentage of the material used on the two new channels must be provided by outside independent production companies, as is currently the case with TV. Remember, a 'production company' can be one freelance journalist with good ideas.

Another opportunity. These stations will be looking for guests to answer calls on phone-in programmes. If you're some sort of specialist or official (Secretary of your local AA perhaps?) you could volunteer. You won't get paid, but you will get expenses, and it's all experience. You never know what it may lead to.

## Regions

As beginners, you might feel as intimidated by national radio networks as by national newspapers. You shouldn't, but for starters why don't you have a crack at the regions?

There are 73 local BBC radio stations in England alone, plus 44 independent stations. Scotland has seven BBC and seven independent; Wales one BBC, three independent; Northern Ireland two BBC, one independent; Guernsey and Jersey one BBC each.

Of those stations, no less than 16 are potentials for journalists in London. The most relevant BBC channel is GLR (Greater London Radio). Then, a little farther out, the BBC has Radios Oxford, Cambridge, Essex, Kent and Sussex.

Additionally, there are the independents – Capital Radio, LBC and Radio 210 for London news, backed by Chiltern, Essex, County (Surrey), Invicta (Kent), Mercury (Sussex), Southern (also Sussex), and Saxon (Suffolk).

Outside of London, let's look at two BBC and two independent stations:

BBC RADIO SCOTLAND (based in Glasgow). Phil Taylor, Head of News & Current Affairs, told me, 'Opportunities are limited, but we do take freelance reporters on our news and current affairs shifts occasionally. We also run four training posts, three in our Glasgow newsroom and one in Aberdeen. But for each post we have something like 700 applications.' (Stiff competition, but *someone* has to be successful).

RED DRAGON RADIO (based in Cardiff). Phil Mercer, Journalist Presenter, told me: 'Best thing for freelances to do is to send us a tape, or even better, bring it in so we can put a face to the voice. The tape could be a news bulletin or anything unusual.'

BBC RADIO SOLENT (based in Southampton). Stuart Noval, News Reporter, told me: 'We're only very occasionally interested in freelances because a track record in print journalism isn't enough. We're stretched to the limit here and anyone coming into news reporting has got to be able to *do* the job straight away. The best advice is to do what I did – get yourself on to hospital radio to get some experience under your belt. After doing a one-year course in hospital radio I then spent about five years in a hospital in Worthing.' (Nationwide there are 21 hospital radios.)

BRMB RADIO (based in Birmingham). Colin Palmer, News Editor, told me: 'Opportunities for freelances are very limited, but each summer, when people are on holiday, we use freelances as temporary stand-ins. But the only people we will look at already have a track record in some sort of radio journalism and/or a diploma or degree in the same subject.'

# Round the clock

One of the great beauties of radio from the writer's viewpoint is that it's a daily medium broadcast all day and much of the night. *All* night in some cases. That adds up to a huge amount of material needed by the editors in charge of the various regions.

According to their size, each BBC regional station has a large or small number of editors. So, as with newspapers, newsmags and magazines, *they* are the freelance journalist's contacts.

GLR has 20 editors. The chief one is the news editor. This channel doesn't have one features editor. There are 19 specialists in charge of agriculture, arts, books, DIY, education, entertainments, films, gardening, health, local government, motoring, classical music, pop music, politics, religious affairs, shopping, sports, theatre, and travel.

GLR don't have a specific editor for women's interests, but Radio Oxford do.

Some of the smaller stations like Radio Essex, Cambridge, and Chiltern have only one news editor in charge, of every subject. All very similar to a regional newspaper.

You need to compile yourself a list of addresses, telex, fax and telephone numbers of editors on regional stations and producers of national network programmes. How do you think you'd do this? The public reference library has phone directories for the whole country. There's also the *Blue Book of British Broadcasting* and the *Music & TV Yearbook*.

# What do they want?

Let's now get on to the WHAT. What do listeners want? What are regional radio editors looking for?

Local NEWS is the cornerstone of them all. The regional stations aim to provide a service of news and a forum for the discussion of issues in their catchment area. Anything you dig up for your local Press can also be passed on to your regional radio station. So you get two payments.

This is often how freelances break into radio. (Chapters 3 and 4 concentrated on news reporting.)

Regional radio also likes to help develop participation by members of the community in social affairs and activities of all kinds. This is only interviewing and profiles all over again (see Chapters 15, 16 and 17).

All regionals gear their broadcasting to the special needs of listeners in their area. These could be retired people, industrial workers or ethnic groups. There's scope here for any freelance who gets involved with local clubs for teenagers, mothers, OAPs, churchgoers, support groups like the AA, Samaritans, Worldwide Fund for Nature . . . anything at all that interests them.

And don't be too insular. They're not into being concerned about the fact that Mrs Jones' dog was run over. What they relish is juicy court cases, local girl makes good, plus projects and schemes for the residents' benefit.

Very popular are talks on current events spurred by INDIGNATION.

## Local involvement

The whole atmosphere of local stations is much more direct and personal than it can be on national networks. The station manager is autonomous and responsible for his/her own schedules. Budgets are limited and pay for beginner freelances is nominal. But this is the door to bigger things.

Any freelance with an original idea or angle can get a lot of job satisfaction from local radio. You can get much more involved than with your local newspaper. Radio offers the opportunity to take part in the programme and possibly help with the planning and presentation. You don't even have to send them a finished piece; just a short synopsis of your idea is enough for a start. But it must be SOMETHING NEW.

It's the same criterion as for any piece of journalism for any printed publication, your angle must be NEW. What you're suggesting to the local radio station or local newspaper is an aspect that involves a change to the status quo. As you know, journalism is *never* a recap of what exists. Yes, that's needed as background, but the idea, the angle you're selling the editor, is WHAT'S NEW.

Freelance Richard Kelsall described his first experience in *Writers' Monthly:*

I began my work as a freelance radio contributor with BBC Radio Newcastle. I was interested in doing a short piece on teenagers in the context of a lively local arts scene.

I talked over the idea with the controller of programmes in Newcastle, and he put me in touch with the station's education producer.

To my amazement, in next to no time I was offered the loan of a splendid portable Uher recording machine with microphone. Full of youthful vanity I strode through the streets of Newcastle with the BBC logo conspicuous, enjoying the ridiculous fantasy of being an ace roving reporter.

Days later, back at the studios, with 15 minutes of what I considered fairly riveting interviews, I was shown how to edit the best bits to about three minutes.

That was the start. Richard 'got the bug' and was soon contributing pieces weekly. He says: 'When the national commercial stations start up in 1992 it will be interesting to see whether they expand the horizons for the freelance.'

## Read it aloud

Always, ALWAYS, read aloud to yourself what you've written before you submit any complete piece of news or a feature to radio. Use a tape recorder. It must be short, crisp and READABLE. Next, ask someone to read it aloud to you. You need to know how it sounds. Do you create any problems for the reader on the air, like tongue twisters? If your friend stumbles over words, so will the radio presenter.

GLR tell me they prefer not to have to rewrite, but to use the piece straight off.

## Training

There's an inexpensive and really cracking book called *Writing for the BBC*. It's available from the BBC Bookshop, Broadcasting House, Portland Place, London W1A 1AA.

If you get really serious about radio, you could apply for a job with the BBC. They recruit trainees, then farm them out to different stations and programmes. The sort of people they recruit already have track records in the local and national Press, and will very likely have a degree, though I think the only 'qualification' is a driving licence!

The 20-month Local Radio Trainee Reporters Scheme takes 18 recruits a year. The phone number is 071–580 4468. Ask for Journalist Training.

Nine colleges run courses officially recognised by the Joint Advisory Committee for the Training of Radio Journalists. You can get details from the National Union of Journalists if you send a stamped addressed envelope to JACTRJ, c/o The NUJ, Acorn House, 314 Grays Inn Rd, London WC1 8DP.

The London College of Printing also offers excellent courses on radio journalism.

# Chapter 24

# Copyright

- Know your rights
- Definition
- What's not protected: headlines, single words, phrases, ideas, angles, plots
- Establishing copyright
- Vanity presses

> 'I'M always amused when I hear unpublished people worrying about copyright. For seven years I've been trying to write something good enough for someone to steal. But it's never happened.'
>
> ROBERT SKEGLUND, Writer (USA)

JACKETS OFF. Fists up. These are YOUR RIGHTS.

First COPYRIGHT, (Serial Rights in the next chapter). Don't switch off. Your whole future as a writer could be affected by knowing or not knowing at least the basics of these rules.

Because some editors (too many), treat writers like dirt, if you're ignorant of the Copyright Act and Serial Rights you could LOSE A GREAT DEAL OF MONEY.

Also, you're extremely vulnerable to pirating from other writers. Ideas aren't protected under the Copyright Act. Anyone can read your unpublished piece, or, in general conversation you might mention what you're writing – and it's not illegal for another person to steal your idea. Be aware of the risk you take when you send entries to competitions – or to unethical editors.

# Definition

What do you understand by copyright? What is it?

As you know, 'copy' is a word used in publishing to describe 'that which is printed, or to be printed' (including photos and drawings, so it doesn't only mean words). And the Copyright Act applies equally to all three. So, copyright means plainly what it says: *the right to the copy*. In other words, the *owner*, and if you write it, that's you.

That copyright gets a law all of its own is because *writers fought for it*. In Britain, copyright law in its modern sense dates only from 1911. It was made more powerful by amendments in 1956, '68, '71, '82, '83, '84 and '88.

In April 1989 it was replaced by the most potent version to date, which includes electronic copying (photocopying and computer discs). Also, writers can object to the DISTORTION of their work. Prison sentences and fines are now heavier. The whole thing is so complicated you need a lawyer to interpret it. I'm giving you just the main points here.

Copyright is an essential part of marketing. Writers are conned all down the line by everyone who can get away with it, including other writers who haven't the creativity to originate their own copy. The Copyright Act is one of the few legal rights you have. Or multiplicity of rights.

The Act is infringed if, WITHOUT THE ORIGINATOR'S CONSENT, another person copies the written piece as it is or adapts it. Please note that. You can't even make a translation or précis, or turn from direct speech into indirect, or from first person into third. For example, it is now illegal to take a photocopy of a page of this book.

Here's an example of one of the complexities. A newspaper reporter is at a public meeting where there's a speech. If the speaker reads out a written speech, then the copyright is the speaker's. But, if he talks off the cuff, then the newspaper has the copyright in its published report. Do you see the difference?

How much of a piece has to be stolen to constitute an infringement? More than 30 words. But this can vary. It's up to the judge if the case is taken to court.

Do you know how long protection lasts? For the author's lifetime, plus 50 years.

Can copyright be assigned to someone else? Yes, but only in writing, verbally is not sufficient. A nice example is that J. M. Barrie signed over all the rights from *Peter Pan* to the Great Ormond Street Hospital for Children.

In the case of a freelance submitting stolen work to an editor, is the freelance the only one liable to go to jail? No, the editor, publisher, printer and distributor go down with you.

# Complications

There are all sorts of complications when you get into co-authorship, ghostwriting and other anomalies. See the good old *Writers' & Artists' Yearbook*, it has an excellent section on the Copyright Act which goes into far more detail than I can here.

# What's not protected?

### HEADLINES, SINGLE WORDS, PHRASES

Now let's look at something that's not protected – headlines, single words and phrases. This is because they're too short to be considered of literary merit. Pity: there are some ingenious words, probably coined by journalists – Rachmanism, teenager, Sloane Ranger, yuppie, fast lane, glitz, gazump. Unfortunately, they're not protected by the Act. That's one reason they're used so often.

As for headlines, 50 people can write a feature on the financial aspects of swimming the Channel, and they can *all* be called *It Pays to be Wet*. It's quite legal.

And for you writers who are also aspiring novelists – the Copyright Act doesn't stop you calling your next book *War and Peace* or *Gone With the Wind*. However, the publisher would still not accept it. Why? There's what's known as a 'pass off' law. You aren't allowed to present your book in any form that tries to 'pass it off' as something already in print. So, if you're writing a book, before you choose a title check out *British Books in Print* or the *British Library Catalogue*.

Using a pseudonym or actual name already in use comes under this heading too.

## IDEAS, ANGLES, PLOTS

Three other creative results not protected by copyright law are ideas, angles and plots. Protection is only afforded when the work exists in its entirety.

Which is another reason never to go into detail about what you're writing or about to write with a person you don't know well enough to trust. There's nothing to stop them stealing ideas from you. If they can get the piece written before you can then the copyright is theirs.

**Example:** A book was published in 1930 called *Gladiator* by Philip Wylie. It was about a man who possessed superhuman powers. The book was filmed in 1938. The same year, Jerome Siegel and Joseph Schuster invented a comic strip which they called *Superman*. They had appropriated the idea.

# How do you establish copyright?

What does a writer have to do to establish not only copyright, but also its date?

Nothing. In British law, copyright exists the minute you type THE END. Just date a copy and stick it in a drawer. It doesn't even have to be witnessed.

However, as a safeguard, some authors mail themselves a copy of every important piece they write by Registered Post. They leave the envelope sealed (vital, this), so, in any dispute, it can be opened in court. The postmark proves the time and date it was created.

It's possible to register the time and date your piece was originated. In the UK registration is voluntary. In some countries it's obligatory if you want protection. In the States you also have the option, and you can do so as an added precaution. Registration rules vary from country to country. Investigate those applicable to your target country as soon as you start offering your work abroad.

# Vanity presses

A further point on registering work. It is a legal obligation that every book printed in the UK has to be sent to the British Library for registration. All publishers have to do it. If you sink low enough to consider a vanity press, you then become a publisher because you've financed the printing of the work. Then it's your obligation (by law) to send six copies to the British Library.

Do you know what a vanity press is? It's where the writer PAYS for publication. No reputable publisher *ever* asks an author to pay any production costs, or to buy copies.

It's usually poets and novelists who go to this extreme. But non-fiction writers have also been known to fall into the pit, especially those writing textbooks or How-to-do-it books.

The Copyright Act as it affects interviewing, news reporting and writing/researching features is well covered in the excellent book *McNae's Essential Law for Journalists* by Walter Greenwood and Tom Welsh (Butterworths). The eleventh edition (1990) of this easy-to-understand volume was published only two years after the previous edition because the Copyright Act was considerably amended in 1988.

This book also details dozens of other sensitive issues guaranteed to give journalists sleepless nights. These include libel (dealt with briefly in my next chapter), Official Secrets Act 1989, civil rights, journalists naming/not naming sources, race relations, freedom of speech, right of appeal, bankruptcy, breaches of confidence, rape reporting etc.

*McNae's* has a very helpful format. At the end of each chapter it asks the reader test questions – the answers to which are given in the chapter they've just read. Every journalist should have a copy.

# Chapter 25

# More Rights – and Some Wrongs

- Angles and Serials
- All rights
- Through the complexities
- Syndicates
- Libel
- Accusation
- Innuendo
- See *Perfect*
- Hostile reviews

---

'JOURNALISTS forget that in the libel world the onus of proof is on the defendant (the journalist) to prove his innocence. The victim of libel awards is investigative journalism because the laws are so weighted against newspapers.'

ALISTAIR BRETT, Solicitor, News International

---

THIS IS the jam on the bread – your multi-sales, folks.

There are two methods of selling your material more than once. ANGLES and SERIALS. They're entirely different.

(1) ANGLES means taking the same material/information and writing it with a different slant. The approach will usually be dictated by the market. Each piece can contain similar ideas or even quotes, but essentially, each one is individual. We've already covered this.

(2) SERIALS means where you write a piece and sell the original several times without changing a comma. It's this second type I'm covering here.

Selling your work already published to a second publication is more or less money for jam. It's one of the few perks of a journalist's lot.

Let's look at selling UK-published work overseas. It can be very lucrative. Many British authors make far more from overseas sales than from UK ones, when the rates are better. They are higher in the States, for instance.

A word of warning. Watch out for Russia, China, East Europe and a few others; they don't recognise our laws. As far as I know, you're safe in the States, Western Europe and the Commonwealth countries. But check it out.

## All rights

Even if a British, American, West European or Commonwealth country buys WORLD RIGHTS, they still haven't bought the original copyright. That is known as ALL RIGHTS and it stays with you. Unless, of course, you're mad enough to state in writing that you relinquish them. Don't ever do that. No ethical publisher should ask you to sell ALL RIGHTS. If an unethical editor asks you to, then just refuse. Tell him he can have British Rights but that's all. If he insists (or no acceptance) compromise with World Rights – or try another publication.

## Through the complexities

The lovely fact of selling serial rights, of course, is that you don't have to change a single word. You sell your feature over and over again, just as it stands.

What rights have you sold if your brand new piece is accepted by the *Guardian*? First British Serial Rights, or, as it's know in the trade, FBSR. Sensible writers make a point of always stressing which rights they're offering the editor. Put it up at the top of your work's first page along with the number of words, headline and other essentials. On pieces you're writing from now on put FBSR. Also put it on your invoices, of course.

Suppose, instead of selling your brand new baby to the *Guard-*

*ian*, you sell it to *Woman's Journal* or *Gentleman's Quarterly*, what rights have you sold? The same.

OK, so you've sold to one of those three. You now sell it to the *New Yorker* – what have you sold? First North American Serial Rights.

Well – you're on to a good thing. We'll say it's a feature on some revolutionary discovery about conserving rare trees. It's been printed in the UK, also in the States, what can you do with it now?

You decide to try your same, unaltered, work with the *British National Geographical Magazine*. What are you offering them? Second British Serial Rights.

They took it. You're now getting quite cocky. Who else might be interested? You think of *Gardener's Weekly*. What rights are you offering them? Third British.

Then, as America's such a huge country, not everyone takes the *New Yorker*. You look at the *San Francisco Herald* – what do you offer them? Second North American Rights.

You can go on indefinitely offering it to whoever you think might buy it, so long as you make it clear which rights you're offering.

# Syndicates

If all this seems like too much hassle, there are syndicates which specialise in sales of subsequent British rights plus overseas rights.

Point No. 1 – syndicates take a commission of anything from 50 per cent upwards.

Point No. 2 – too many of them just happen to forget to tell you when they've sold your work.

Syndicates are nothing more than marketing companies. There are no more magazines and newspapers open to them than to the writer. Their skill is knowing what editors want in various countries, including the UK.

After you've considered the odds, make up your own mind on syndicates. Marketing is something someone else can do for you, whereas writing isn't. You can perhaps better deploy your time by creating new stuff.

If they'll take your work they will very likely sell it. And these will be sales you wouldn't otherwise have (despite that painful 50 to 60 per cent cut).

How's this for an anecdote I heard quite a few years back now? Cartoonist Frank Dickens, who does *Bristow* for the London *Evening Standard*, only got £10 per strip, per day, ie £50 a week. *But* the same strips are syndicated daily in something like 150 other publications worldwide. Now do some mental arithmetic . . .

A penultimate word on syndicates from the *Writers' & Artists' Yearbook*: 'In their own interests writers are *strongly* advised to make preliminary enquiries *before* submitting MSS to syndicates, and to ascertain terms of work.'

And a last word from me on YOUR RIGHTS TO SYNDICATE – they're included in ALL RIGHTS. Read all the small print on any contract you receive from an editor. Ensure you're not selling your right to syndicate along with everything else.

# Libel

This is the bad news. The libel law means all sorts of agonies for the uninformed journalist. If you contravene it you could be blacklisted by editors – in addition to the sentence from the judge!

What is it? Or to put it another way, when is slander libel? It's WRITTEN defamation. The criteria used by juries in court are:

(1) Does the matter complained of tend to lower the plaintiff in the estimation of society?
(2) Does it tend to bring him into hatred, ridicule, contempt, dislike or disesteem with society?
(3) Does it tend to make him shunned or avoided or cut off from society?

Note this next bit well – the mere fact that what was published might be ACCURATE would not absolve the writer. It's the EFFECT the statement has on the plaintiff that's actionable.

Neither can you get away with irony. Brutus, had he been alive at the time, would have had a watertight case against Shakespeare for writing: 'But Brutus is an honourable man'.

And you don't necessarily have to name the victim. A corrup-

tion of his name, a nickname or an accurate description of his
physical appearance, job or habits is enough. Be aware of the many
pitfalls.


# Accusation

Reporting news has its risks. Even if you're professional and stick
to the facts.

**Example:** You could cover a pretty ordinary story. This necessi-
tates interviewing a couple who have two kids whose home has
been burgled four times in as many months. While talking to them
it's casually mentioned that the parents aren't married. But *don't
say so in print*. That can be interpreted as ACCUSATION. You're
libelling the kids by insinuating they're illegitimate.

Anyway, the fact that the parents aren't married has nothing
whatsoever to do with the burglaries. It's only a journalist who has
an ambition to work in the gutter press who would find a way of
bringing in this point.

And be extra careful reporting a crime that has been committed.
The juiciest bits are usually written *after* the court case. As you
would expect, the gutter press give it the works, but they write
with a lawyer at their elbow. (And they still get it wrong!)

By the way, it would be quite OK to print the words 'Henry
VIII was a lecher and murderer'. You can't libel the dead.

Editors hate amateurs because they're frightened of their
unprofessional attitude. Amateurs don't check and recheck facts.
Their inexperience can get publications into serious trouble.

**Example:** A male VIP attends a civic function. It's reported in
the local Press. There was a woman with the VIP, so the beginner
reporter writes: 'Mr Baker arrived at the function with his wife.'

She wasn't his wife. She was his mistress. His wife has every
right to sue the paper. And she'd win. Reporters must *never* make
assumptions. If you're too lazy or too irresponsible to CHECK FACTS
you shouldn't be in the business.

# Innuendo

Just because it *did* happen or *was* said is not enough reason to print it. A neophyte reporter could land the paper with a suit for libel by INNUENDO.

**Example:** In this story the journalist wrote: 'When Peter Brown was asked whether John Smith was a suitable and responsible person to take charge of the boys' home, Brown smiled and wouldn't answer.'

Can you see the malicious innuendo there? Smith may be a highly moral and responsible person but, unknown to the reporter, Brown hates his guts because Smith beat him at squash that week. So when he is interviewed by a freelance reporter for their local paper, Brown sees a subtle way of kneeing Smith in the groin.

You must think twice – three times – about anything like this that you write. Can it possibly be misconstrued? Look at it through the eyes of the person you're writing about. Also, would you like this to be written about *you*? Don't go for a cheap thrill at someone else's expense. Those are gutter press tactics. They don't let facts get in the way of a good story.

In *all* cases adopt the journalist's golden rule: IF IN DOUBT, LEAVE IT OUT. Don't take chances.

Not only do you risk your professional integrity as a journalist, but libel can severely damage your bank balance. Editors don't pay a freelance journalist's court costs. And it isn't only if you're guilty. Even if you win, a libel action can still bankrupt you.

You can insure against being served a writ for libel. Insurance schemes are operated by the Institute of Journalists and the National Union of Journalists.

# See *Perfect*

More than once a person has had a nervous breakdown or committed suicide after being written about by a journalist. Would you like blood on your hands? As I've mentioned before – be very well aware of the power of the pen.

For students of journalism I think the film *Perfect* (available on video) should be obligatory viewing. It stars Jamie Lee Curtis and John Travolta. It's a serious story, not a musical. The hero is a journalist who develops a major problem – which you'll all meet. The problem is the lengths to which a journalist will go for a good story, the way he writes it up and the repercussions for the people he interviews.

In the film Travolta works for *Rolling Stone*, an incisive American magazine that actually exists in real life. (Stan Nicholls, the journalist I interview in this book, has been printed in it.) The film is a semi-documentary as some of the characters are real – the editor, for instance, and the girl photographer.

*Perfect* gives both sides of the story. Do try and see it. It'll give you plenty of heart-searching.

## Hostile reviews

Many unkind things are said by reviewers. The difference between the professional and the amateur is that they know how to stay within the bounds of the libel law. It decrees that OPINION is not libellous, but ACCUSATION is.

**Example:** 'Nellie Smith's performance of Ophelia was extremely wooden', is considered the opinion of the critic. 'Peter Smith's performance of Joe, the alcoholic, was very convincing; probably because of his personal predilection for the hard stuff', is considered accusation.

There's quite a subtle difference. But thousands of juries have spent thousands of hours sorting out subtleties.

Mark this: OPINION has to be RELEVANT. There was a case where a Sunday tabloid critic wrote that a particular actress had a big nose. The actress said this was a personal affront, and took the paper to court. She won. In the critic's OPINION she *did* have a big nose. But the point the judge upheld was that it wasn't fair comment on her *stage performance*. It wasn't RELEVANT.

And who do you think is penalised – the author alone? No, the editor, publisher, printer and distributor are equally guilty. This is one of the major reasons editors are always WARY OF AMATEURS and hesitate to accept their copy.

OK, yes, I know *Private Eye* thrives despite libel cases, so does Rupert Murdoch's *Sun*. They spend millions on defending charges. Do you remember dear Rupert using his entire front page to apologise to the Queen? There was also the unprecedented, massive front page banner headline saying SORRY ELTON to Elton John. But their purses are deeper than yours.

A survey of court cases reveals that libel writs are seldom about front-page biggies. They're mostly about those minor, inside page stories which journalists dash off in a state of frantic anxiety because the deadline looms.

If you want to be a journalist, you can't work without learning a goodly chunk of the law of libel. There are quite detailed explanations in the *Writers' & Artists' Yearbook* and the *Writer's Handbook*.

# Chapter 26

# Technology for The Terrified

- Dictating/recording machine
- Word processor
- Telephone answering machine
- Facsimile
- Laptop
- Camera
- Radio

---

'I'M all in favour of newspapers and publishers being sympathetic to new writers. But I don't think you can have an organised system of government (financial) help. Writers just have to get along with it.'

ROY HATTERSLEY, Journalist and former Deputy Leader of the Labour Party

---

ASSUMING you may be as big a technophobe as I am, this chapter is written as simply as possible. It's a brief rundown on a few devices essential for a successful journalist and contains no jargon.

A journalist equipped only with a typewriter and Biro is as out-dated as one with a quill pen. To survive in today's fiercely competitive journalistic arena you need to invest in at least four user-friendly aids – a dictating machine, a word processor, a telephone answering machine and a fax. Each means GREATER SPEED for the same physical effort – plus CONVENIENCE and ACCURACY.

# Dictating/recording machine

I've already mentioned tape recorders in Chapter 15. It's said we speak seven times faster than we can write. Even if you can write shorthand at 90 words per minute (the average), you'll have difficulty keeping up with a speaker for any length of time.

A cassette recorder is invaluable for taping ACCURATE quotes/speeches/lectures. You're competing against other journalists who *will* have tape recorders, so your editor can check the accuracy of your written words against those printed in other publications covering the same story.

The machine has other uses too. Use it as a notebook to record ideas/angles/headlines. And you can record telephone calls using a small acoustic coupler linked to your recorder.

I have a Sanyo dictating machine which cost just over £30. It works on batteries and mains. It's cheaper to use electricity when doing those lengthy transcriptions. A one-hour interview can take five hours to transcribe into text.

When buying one always test its recording range. For interviewing you will be sitting close to your subject, but if you're at a lecture and the front row is full up, will it pick up the speaker from several rows back?

Ensure you get a reliable after-sales service.

# Word processor

Today quite a number of editors are insisting that contributions are submitted on disc, not on paper. It's only a matter of time before the majority of publications go over to this method.

It makes sense. It saves them having to re-set (re-type) your copy. They merely put your disc in their machine and the text comes up on their screen. Anything to save time and cost in this competitive world.

And, from the journalists' viewpoint, it's extra money. Copy on disc gets a higher rate than that on paper.

Like several thousand other journalists, I use a modest Amstrad. Mine's a 9512 – not IBM compatible, so its discs can't be accepted by all editors. (Amstrad do an IBM-compatible model.)

But this, and the other disadvantage of not being very fast, is far outweighed by its advantages.

1   It's good value for money – and the price included a daisywheel printer plus the softwear (program) to run it. (With some WPs you have to buy these as extras.)

2   Discs to hold the text, and ribbons for the printer aren't expensive. And it uses the same A4 size paper as a typewriter.

3   It has a very user-friendly manual which teaches you how to operate it. You're taken via a series of tutorials through all the facilities the Amstrad offers.

4   Unlike a typewriter, you can edit on screen. This saves you laboriously typing out the whole feature every time you make an alteration. Making three, four or more drafts is easy.

5   It will check the spelling of 80,000 words – plus those you enter yourself.

6   It will count the number of words.

It has many other facilities – test drive one in a shop.

Members of the National Union of Journalists and Institute of Journalists can get a discount on Amstrads, and on other makes. I'm using the Amstrad as an example merely because it's the one of which I have most experience.

There are several other makes (just as there are when buying a car), some with their special discounts. Here we go again – do your market research – then go to a reputable dealer. Don't make the mistake of buying an expensive one that sings, dances and puts the cat out. Very few journalists need more than the word processing facility.

And take out a service contract – mine is with Dictaphone. If anything goes wrong they will have an engineer with me the next day. If you don't have a contract, the engineer will still come, but contract customers have precedence.

# Telephone answering machine

Even though you're at home, an answering machine is a useful method of filtering out the phone calls you don't wish to receive from those you do. It also makes sure you're not interrupted when you need to get down to writing.

A journalist colleague said: 'Mine paid for itself in the first week. I was out when the *Daily Mail* rang asking me to do a story. I was able to return their call – and I got the commission. If I hadn't had the machine the commission would have gone to someone else.

'I have a Remote Control with mine. Wherever I am, even abroad, I can contact my answering machine and it will play back messages. This is a fantastic advantage – again, it ensures I get vital messages fast.'

A word of caution: answering machines can increase your phone bill. Why? Because you will have to do the phoning back. A way around this is to keep the volume control turned up so you can hear who is calling, then simply pick up the receiver if it's someone to whom you wish to speak.

# Facsimile

Owning a fax (short for facsimile) means you can be writing right up to minutes before the deadline. All other ways of getting the copy to the editor take longer.

A fax is simply a device that transmits a photocopy. What the recipient receives is a facsimile of what you put in at your end. So you retain the original as a record. Apart from pure text, it can transmit maps and graphs.

A fax bureau will transmit for you – at a substantial price per page *plus* a flat fee. So you don't need to have your machine long before it pays for itself.

Ideally, to operate a fax machine, you need an additional line from British Telecom. This isn't always necessary, it depends on the model – check with the dealer or BT. Beware of cheap models. What you can't see in the shop when you buy it is the state of the piece of paper your recipient gets. If it's illegible, eg splodgy, faint or has some text missing, then you're not the editor's friend.

If you're sending a 2,000 word feature, that's at least eight A4-size pages, so an automatic paper feeder can be useful. (But additional gimmicks are additional functions that can go wrong!)

You will always need a home-based fax, if only for receiving messages when you're out, but if you're a roving reporter, a mobile fax is useful in your car. And see my comments on laptops.

# Laptop

Some time or other you'll possibly jettison the word processor you have on your desk for a portable one, a Laptop or Notepad. Or you may prefer to have a desk (standard) model plus a lightweight one you can take when you go on roving commissions. In the old days of typewriters most journalists had a standard model and a portable. It makes sense to have a machine you can take with you, enabling you to write on trains and planes. (Or in the lavatory immediately after conducting your interview!)

Either Laptop or Notepad machines are only a little larger than a telephone directory, and can have a bubble jet printer of about the same size. They are light enough to be not too much of a problem for women journalists.

A colleague, a foreign correspondent for a number of newspapers, swears by his Toshiba T1000LE Laptop. This has all the functions of my Amstrad standard model. In addition, because he uses a Mercury LINK 7500 line, his Laptop will send text, via its modem, straight to an editor's computer – wherever he is in the world. He doesn't need to post a disc.

Other plus points are that through his Laptop he can link up with various data bases and libraries when he's doing research.

Its screen shows 25 lines of text at a time, and it can be operated by re-chargeable batteries or mains electricity.

His Laptop can send messages and copy to any telex or fax number worldwide. It also gives him a telex number and a 'mailbox' where messages for him are kept till he asks for them to be displayed on his screen.

Capabilities and prices of Laptops vary enormously – shop around. Again, several makers of Laptop offer journalists discounts – call the manufacturer's PR department.

And here are two pieces of not-so-new technology:

# Camera

An inexpensive, automatic, compact, 35mm camera with a built-in flash is essential for mug shots (portraits) of people you interview. You don't need anything more sophisticated (and expensive) such as motordrives, extra lenses and tripods – you're not competing with bona fide Press photographers.

As well as the simplicity, small size and light weight of a compact camera, there are other advantages. They're powered by batteries and use films that are easily available. You can buy them in chemists and newsagents as well as photographic shops.

# Radio

If you're a reporter on the move you need to know how situations are developing, so get a tiny short wave radio. It's useful to be able to tune in to news programmes.

Do remember that all this equipment not only adds to your efficiency, it is also tax deductible as a business expense. Your accountant will be able to tell you about this.

# Chapter 27

# Loneliness of the Long-suffering Journalist

- Writers' clubs
- Writers' associations
- Trade Press
- Self-discipline
- Tenacity
- Confidence
- Further training
- Self-help
- Round up of recommended books

---

'EDUCATION is never as expensive as ignorance.'

Chinese Proverb

---

WRITING dictates that I work in isolation. I don't know any freelance writer who doesn't. So, unlike people who work in offices, shops or factories, we lack the stimulation and support of others.

But there's a degree of gregarious dependence deep, deep down programmed genetically into every one of us. However self-sufficient we are, all of us benefit from some contact with other wordsmiths.

## Writers' clubs

For creative people who have to work alone one of the best ways of finding birds of a feather is to join a Writers' Club. There's a national *Directory of Writers' Clubs* updated annually by Jill Dick.

Good-standard writers' clubs can be a tremendous amount of help to non-established writers, and established ones too. That is if you can read out your written work for constructive criticism. Many clubs do this.

Reading work aloud is a valuable exercise.

Many professionals read their work aloud to themselves before sending it to editors. It gives them a different perspective on the piece. While reading, the author gets an objective view. Even if you can't read it out for others to criticise, it's a good idea to read it into a tape recorder then play it back. This helps you spot awkward phrases, overlong sentences and other amateur touches.

Constructive criticism from other writers is extremely valuable. Before you read out your opus ask your audience to comment on market suitability (show them the publication you're aiming at), flow, credibility and tenses. Is it informative? Is it easily understood? Are sentences too long? Are there any superfluous words? Did they LEARN SOMETHING NEW? Is the style 'alive' or is it dull (because it's only book research rehashed)?

When you hear other people's work read out you learn to develop your own analytical faculties – 'That's a good angle' or 'What a mess, I'll know not to do that in my piece'. It teaches you how to judge your own work. Nobody writes successfully until they can see their own creations objectively.

Even though many other people at the writers' club may be amateurs, remember they are also READERS. You will be getting comments from a cross-section of the reading public.

If you feel nervous about reading to others, practise at home.

Criticism hurts. Of course it does. But it will point out factors you've probably missed. They're not criticising *you*, just your work; and that you can rewrite. The old adage about not being able to see the wood for the trees applies here. So go along to the club prepared to accept the criticism dispassionately.

And don't forget to make detailed notes of *everything* that's said so you can assess them at home afterwards. When by yourself you can decide which comments are valid and which aren't.

Writers need to be able to exchange ideas and experiences with others. It's a very solitary profession. The only people who genuinely understand the problems and complexities of being a writer are other writers.

# Writers' associations

We need all the help we can get. Joining an association gives you credibility. Benefits include: trade union muscle, legal advice, negotiations on fees and contracts, interaction with established writers and ENCOURAGEMENT.

Criterion for full membership is always based on having work already in print, but many have associate membership for beginners. They mainly have London addresses, but many have regular regional meetings and send out their own newsletters or journals.

When making enquiries ALWAYS enclose a decent size (A5 at least), stamped addressed envelope.

**SOME USEFUL ADDRESSES:**
Institute of Journalists, 2 Dock Offices, Surrey Quays, Lower Road, London SE16 2XL *Tel: 071–252 1187*
National Union of Journalists, Acorn House, 314 Grays Inn Road, London WC1X 8DP *Tel: 071–278 7916*
Pen International (British Branch), 7 Dilke Street, London SW3 4JE *Tel: 071–352 6303*
Society of Authors, 84 Drayton Gardens, London SW10 9SB *Tel: 071–373 6642*
Society of Women Writers and Journalists, Jean Hawkes (Hon. Sec.), 110 Whitehall Road, Chingford, London E4 6DW.

Look in the *Writers' & Artists' Yearbook* for more.

# Trade Press

If you're serious about becoming a journalist you'll get a great deal of help from your trade publications. You also keep up with modern journalistic style because this is the language used in these publications.

This is how you get advance information. *UK Press Gazette* (071–583 6463) gives you up-to-date news on forthcoming publication launches, revamps, changes of direction and new projects of established ones, what editors are doing, which publications they're moving to, and job vacancies.

*Writers' Monthly* (0881–888 1242) gives useful tips for beginners, straight-from-the-horse's-mouth experiences and market news.

Only a few newsagents stock these. Better to ask for a sample edition, then take out a subscription (ask them how much) and have it mailed to you direct.

## Self-discipline

Writing in the *Sunday Times*, the author J. B. Priestley said:

> Any successful writer needs tremendous self-discipline. He must be in control of his own attitudes of mind and his actions. He has to compel himself to work steadily and do his best. Nobody else can make him do it – not even his publisher, not even his wife. Day after day he must go to his desk and face the icy challenge of the blank paper. And when all is done, when his work is published, he must stand there naked in the market place waiting for applause or rotten eggs. Believe me, it takes self-discipline.

I have an appalling memory, so as a structured part of my self-discipline I need to write notes to myself and pin them up. These reminders are for things like deadlines, notes to ring editors to ask why my piece wasn't in Tuesday's edition as they promised, notes to chase payments, notes to update my record of daily expenses.

## Tenacity

Tenacity can be interpreted as another word for self-discipline. You often need the organisation and persistence of the Mafia to get your work published.

**Example:** How's this for tenacity? When Abraham Lincoln was a young man he ran for the legislature in Illinois and was badly trounced. He next entered a business, failed, and spent 17 years paying the debts of a worthless partner.

Lincoln became candidate for the United States Senate, but was badly defeated. In 1856 he tried again – and again failed. And in 1858 he was defeated by Douglas.

One failure after another – great setbacks. Yet he became one of the greatest men America ever had, before or since. What he *did* have was faith in himself.

**Example:** Richard Adams' *Watership Down* was turned down scores of times before it was published – and John Braine's *Room at the Top* 24 times. Both were eventually best-sellers.

As for journalism – *all* editors are genuinely desperate for new writers. What they're NOT looking for is AMATEUR writers. Learn your trade first.

# Confidence

So often students confide that they lack confidence. Lack of confidence is self-doubt. If you don't have doubt, in other words, if you're sure what you have to sell is up to professional standard – THAT gives you confidence.

Building confidence is tantamount to learning how to judge what's 'good' journalism, then learning how to write it and how to sell it.

The only way to assess good, modern journalism is to read, read and then read some more. Fresh examples appear in the Press daily; there's no lack of opportunities to see what editors accept.

*You* don't need to be told 'that's a good piece'. You know whether it told you something new, and was written in an interesting, entertaining manner with an original use of words.

Whenever you feel agreeably satisfied after you've read a piece, cut it out for reference. You might have said: 'Well, I didn't know that before', or 'She's got a really good argument there', or 'That's a clever alternative to a cliché'. Aim to emulate.

As for writing professional-standard stuff yourself, that's what part of this book is about – learning the 'how'. What the rest of the book is about is selling it.

I give you the ingredients but you have to make them into the cake. Practise, practise, practise builds up confidence.

# Further training

GET AS MUCH JOURNALISTIC TRAINING AS YOU CAN. Reading this book is a commendable start. But there are also courses on becoming a journalist. You'll progress faster if you immerse yourself in the subject. No book or course can cover every single factor – you'll learn something new from each source.

However, a word of warning. The field of journalistic training has more than its share of risks. There are plenty of sharks exploiting people's egos. Like it or not, inherent in all creative pursuits is the ego trip. We're all on one. There are con men who know this and exploit the gullible. Hence, beware of SOME correspondence courses, and of SOME writing schools.

But local council Adult Education courses are not out to exploit the students. Every September there's a choice of day and evening classes starting. Some last the three terms (autumn, winter, summer), some, like mine, run for one term only, so you can start in September, January or April. And they're real value for money as they're subsidised by the council. Look for classes specifically on JOURNALISM – those entitled *Creative Writing* are definitely not the same thing.

Exploitation is also another name for VANITY PRESSES. You PAY a publisher to print your work. You'll see adverts for them. The vanity presses are strictly for amateurs and people whose work is sub-standard. (See page 199.)

An exception, perhaps, is poetry. It's difficult to get poems published any other way. And yes, James Joyce had to pay a publisher to print *Ulysses*. You merely have to read it to discover why.

By the way, don't confuse vanity presses with *self-publishing*. This is when an author goes into desk-top publishing and prints his own work. He also DISTRIBUTES the publication to retailers.

## TRAINING CENTRES

Bristol Polytechnic, St Mathias, Oldbury Court Road, Fishponds, Bristol BS16 2JP *Tel: 0272 656261*   Broadcast journalism, one-year course.

City University, Frobisher Crescent, London EC2Y 8HB *Tel: 071–628 5641* Post-grad courses in newspaper, radio and periodical journalism, all one year.

College of Technology, Cleveland Avenue, Darlington, Co. Durham *Tel: 0325 467651* Newspaper journalism, one year, pre-entry; International Diploma in Journalism, one year, for students from overseas.

Falmouth School of Art & Design, Wood Lane, Falmouth, Cornwall TR11 4RA *Tel: 0326 211077* Radio journalism, one year, post-grad entry.

Harlow College, Journalism Division, East Site, The Hides, Netteswell, Harlow, Essex CM20 3RA *Tel: 0279 441288* Newspaper journalism, one year, pre-entry.

Highbury College of Technology, Cosham, Portsmouth, Hants PO6 2SA *Tel: 0705 383131* Newspaper journalism, one year, post-grad pre-entry.

Lancashire Polytechnic, Colonial Buildings, Preston, Lancs PR1 2TQ *Tel: 0772 201201* Newspaper journalism, one year, post-grad pre-entry (includes TV).

London College of Printing, Elephant and Castle, London SE1 6SB *Tel: 071–735 8484* Periodical journalism, one year, pre-entry; one term, post-grad. Radio journalism, post-grad/mature students one-year CNAA Diploma.

Media Production Services, Ferndale Road, London SW9 8EJ *Tel: 071–737 7152* TV journalism, one-year diploma and three-month certificate courses.

Napier College, Dept of Print, Media, Publishing & Communications, 219 Colinton Road, Edinburgh EH14 1DJ *Tel: 031–444 2266* HND journalism across the media studies, two years.

PMA Publishing Services, The Old Anchor, Church Street, Hemingford Grey, Cambs PE18 9DF *Tel: 0480 496022* Periodical journalism, short courses.

Periodicals Training Council, Imperial House, 15–19 Kingsway, London WC2B 6UN *Tel: 071–836 8798* Editorial short courses.

Polytechnic of Central London, School of Communications, 18–22 Riding House Street, London W1P 7PD *Tel: 071–486 5811* Radio, one year, pre-entry for ethnic minority students.

Stradbroke College of Further Education, Spinkhill Drive, Shef-
field S13 8FD *Tel: 0742 392621*   Newspaper journalism, one
year, pre-entry.
The Training Department, Paramount House, 104–108 Oxford
Street, London W1N 9FA *Tel: 071–580 6312*   Short courses
on subbing and editorial management.
University of Wales, Journalism Studies, 69 Park Place, Cardiff
CF1 3AS  *Tel: 0222 874000*  Post-grad  one-year  diploma.
Options on media.
Vauxhall College, Dept of Continuing Education, Belmore Street,
London SW8 2JY *Tel: 071–498 1234*   Introduction to journal-
ism 'from a black perspective', one-year, part-time, over-20s.

The twice-yearly directory *Time to Learn* lists approximately 30
writing courses held in colleges and centres in different parts of the
UK and abroad. Lengths of these study breaks vary from a day or
weekend to a week or more. Cost of the directory is £2, including
postage & packaging, from National Institute of Adult Continuing
Education, 19b De Montfort Street, Leicester LE1 7GE.

# Self-help

There's a dearth of textbooks on journalism. Hunt the public
libraries. Browse in the large bookshops. You can get hold of
books on the craft of article writing, but they're not really what
you need if you want to be sure of selling your work.

Some professional and useful books are list on page 222,
together with recommended reference books.

If you send a stamped addressed envelope you can get an
excellent list of textbooks from London Media Workshops, 101
Kings Drive, Gravesend, Kent DA12 5BQ *Tel: 0474 564676*.

# Round up of Recommended Books

## Reference
These are all updated annually and can be found in your local public library, but best to buy your own:

*Benn's Media Directory*, 2 vols (Benn), includes regional and trade press
*Pear's Cyclopaedia* (Pelham)
*Whitaker's Almanack* (J. Whitaker & Sons)
*Willings' Press Guide* (Reed Information Services), comprehensive worldwide media info on 3,600 newspapers, 15,200 periodicals and 2,300 annuals.
*Writers' & Artists' Yearbook* (A. & C. Black), published October.
Barry Turner, *The Writers' Handbook* (Macmillan), published October

## General

Malcolm Bird, *How to Collect the Money You are Owed* (Piatkus)
Dorothea Brande, *Becoming a Writer* (Macmillan)
Andrew Crofts, *How to Make Money from Freelance Writing* (Piatkus)
Harold Evans, *Editing and Design*, 5 vols (Macmillan), a manual of English, typography and layout, published for the National Council for the Training of Journalists. Most useful to aspiring journalists are Book 1, *Newsman's English*, and Book 3, *News Headlines*
H.W. Fowler, *A Dictionary of Modern English Usage* (OUP)
Walter Greenwood & Tom Welsh, *McNae's Essential Law for Journalists* (Butterworths)
Ann Hoffmann, *Research for Writers* (A. & C. Black)
Paul Kerton, *The Freelance Writer's Handbook* (Ebury Press)
Raymond Murphy, *Essential Grammar in Use (With Answers)* (CUP)
Leslie Sellers, *The Simple Sub's Book* (Pergamon)
Keith Waterhouse, *Waterhouse on Newspaper Style* (Viking)
E.S.C. Weiner, *The Oxford Miniguide to English Usage* (OUP)

# Chapter 28

# Rewards and Risks

- Rewards
- . . . And the risks

- Opportunities: one
  career example

---

'WE look for writers, qualified in their subject, who are dedicated enough to research thoroughly and write snappy, interesting copy.'

LAURA VITALE, Editor, *Better Health & Living* (USA)

---

## Rewards

I ADDED several noughts to my bank balance by specialising in heavy industry. Unusual for a woman? Not any more.

My initial impetus was an insatiable 'How do they make that? – design that? – discover that?' This is a marvellous way of being PAID for what you're keen to discover anyway.

Aluminium, oil, pharmaceuticals, stationery and office equipment were my specialist areas. Apart from the lovely lucre, I was taken to places the general public don't see – a smelting plant (spectacular, awesome), photo gravure/polymer laminate printing plant (sheer brilliant hi-tech), laboratory animal houses (emotive!).

And the glamour. Yes the press *do* go on glorious freebies in helicopters and yachts. I had enough daily press reception invites to stuff food and drink till my legs and liver collapsed. The high incidence of obesity and alcohol addiction among journalists bears witness! (But I became so concerned by it all, I'm now one of the very few teetotal journalists in captivity.)

And there are other rewards. One of the IPC women's magazines was approached by an ex-student of mine. The editor was so enthusiastic about her idea for a feature that she paid for her to go to Bali to get the background details.

I heard about this only six months after she'd left my course on journalism. It's always gratifying to have a student contact you to tell about successes. I'm a little sad that, with you being a reader, I don't have any direct contact with you.

Freelances can make more money than staffers. But only if they get all their pieces accepted. All the copy written by staffers is accepted because they work directly for the editor and have a detailed brief.

Many staffers have been tempted by the big money a freelance can make. Some are brave enough to chuck in their jobs. But it's very cold out there (out here, I should say) in the big wide world. The uphill slog of selling to editors can annihilate ex-staffers' confidence permanently. Often they go burrowing back and ask for their old jobs.

A colleague of mine states categorically that he'd never do a staff job. For one thing, he wouldn't give up that mind-blowing marvellous feeling when you're accepted. He describes it thus: 'It's akin to jumping off a cliff, flapping your arms – *and you actually fly.*' I agree 200 per cent.

He also likes the freedom. To wear what you want, for instance. In the winter you can sit writing wrapped in a duvet with your feet on the dog. In the summer, when staff writers are sweating in their supposed-to-be-air-conditioned offices, a freelance can write in the nude.

Freedom also includes choosing your own hours. Why be chained to 9 to 5? Most of the successful freelances I know work from ten in the morning to two the next morning!

And then there's the reverse of the coin, says my colleague. Apart from firemen, he can't think of any other calling where you're perpetually cliff-hanging. Journalists have only their wits between them and bankruptcy. You're only as good as your last idea. Few of my colleagues have any fingernails left – can they pull yet ANOTHER idea out of their head?

Agonising? Yes. But not one of them would do anything else, it seems.

## . . . And the risks

So much is stacked against freelance journalists. They are double losers. If they send in a cracking idea to an editor, they risk it being pirated. If they don't send it in they don't eat.

Thankfully pirating is rare, but one or two newspapers and magazines are low enough to steal ideas from writers. Even editors of well-known, popular publications.

Yes, I know names, but I can't give them because they have better lawyers than I can afford.

One of the advantages of joining a writers' club or association (see Chapter 27) is the NETWORKING when members meet up. They swap experiences and broadcast the names of editors economical with ethics. This, of course, serves a similar function to the editors' network where they warn each other about unreliable freelances.

Another hazard – I've devoted an entire chapter to how slow many publications are at paying you.

And another ethical point – this time on your side. Say you have the chance of interviewing a person everyone wants to read about. Two or three editors in the same field have asked you for the profile. Do you sell it to all of them? It's lots of lovely unethical money. Or do you tell all but one, 'Sorry, but I've already sold it'?

This is a short-term versus long-term thing. If you sell the profile more than once, and all at the same time, you get short-term money. But when those profiles are published and the editors see how they've been duped, guess who never works for any of them again?

## Opportunities: one career example

Many professional journalists earn a bit extra as stringers (occasional freelance reporters) for a local paper, and carry on throughout their career. Habit dies hard if you've developed a nose for news. They also earn pin money stringing for the nationals. I do.

Journalism leads up all sorts of fascinating and lucrative avenues. As just one example you might like to know how my career developed.

As with thousands of professional journalists, I started as an editorial assistant – courtesy title for cub reporter/typist/general dogsbody. I worked on the official journal of a trade association. There were just the two of us, the editor and I.

I'd been there three months when the editor's wife rang to say her husband was in hospital in a meningitis coma. That's when I *really* discovered the meaning of panic.

I had to learn fast. There was nobody to ask. I brought out the next edition winging it and doing lots of agonising, swearing and praying. I remember sleeping at the office several nights when press day loomed.

My editor was unconscious for two months and didn't come back to work for six more. By then I'd got the hang of things and was writing and producing every edition – on deadline.

My poor editor's illness dramatically compressed my learning process. Traumatic; but I loved every minute.

Journalists tend not to stay in one place too long but extend their experience by changing jobs quite frequently. I moved from there to IPC Business Press (part of the *Daily Mirror* group) as a news features editor.

There were dozens of trade journals in the same building as mine, which gave me the opportunity to learn more about my trade. Always having had a yen for design, while with IPC I picked up page make-up. So I became a layout artist as well.

After some years in the stationery Trade Press I got the urge to be more creative and launch a newspaper of my own design. I agree with Ian Watson, editor of *The European*, Europe's first national newspaper, launched May 1990: 'In every journalist's heart lies the desire to edit a paper.'

But I still needed experience as a full-blown editor. I liked the sound of a vacancy I saw for an editor in heavy industry, so took the job. Industrial journalism gets you behind the scenes in factories and laboratories.

My first stab at launching a tabloid was as a newly appointed editor in a multi-national aluminium company. But the trade unions objected. There were ten represented in that company and they wanted the exclusive right to give information to employees. They decreed there mustn't be direct communication between management and staff. My paper carried news of what was going on in the company, in the board room, in the laboratories, in the offices, on the shop floor. It reported on company products, manufacturing methods, staff amenities and appointments. The shop stewards blacked it. They destroyed each edition as it was produced so that it wouldn't reach employees. So I moved on.

Another multi-national company, in the pharmaceutical industry this time, needed a tabloid launched. This I did. During my years with them I added a magazine, audio-visuals plus an annual financial report. The report won a national award for two years running. It did, in fact, achieve the hat trick, but by then was being produced by my erstwhile assistant editor, sitting in my chair. I'd been made redundant.

I plunged into freelancing as a consultant editor/journalist/designer. Since being made redundant I've launched two newspapers and two magazines – all for different companies. Additionally, I'm a news correspondent for an oil company, and regular correspondent for an American tourist magazine. In between, I write for women's magazines and national dailies like the *Guardian* and *Independent*.

All this developed from starting on the lowest rung in a trade journal . . . and before that from merely having the urge to write and going on a course to learn how.

It's a planned career and went exactly as I wanted it to. Yes, I was made redundant. But I'd already had a studio built on to my house and installed a desk, word-processor and filing cabinet. My employer merely brought forward my move into freelancing by a few months.

My very modest career has given me the opportunity to do a lot of travelling, visit hundreds of fascinating places and meet as many interesting people. I can honestly say I get 200 per cent job satisfaction. As for financial reward – I have my own house and over the last couple of years have spent a few months travelling in Nepal, India, China, Java and Tibet at my own expense.

For me, journalism is the most fulfilling, exciting and challenging career there is.

# Answers to Exercises

## ANSWER TO EXERCISE 3

| WHO | WHAT | WHERE | WHEN | WHY | HOW |
|---|---|---|---|---|---|
| Nigel Trent | protested | Piccadilly | Yesterday | Against nuclear weapons | Flew banner |
| Police | want info | Wolver-hampton | Yesterday | Riot after drugs raid | Set up hotlines |
| Children | can be helped | Britain | Today | Emotion-ally disturbed | Read book on Marilyn |
| Hampstead Crime Prevention Squad | help sex victims | West Hampstead | Soon (implied by 'is compiling') | High risk area | Compiled survey |

## ANSWER TO EXERCISE 4

*This is one version only of how the story can be written*

A man was killed on the M1 near Whitechester on 18 November when his Ford Escort skidded into the River Swift. When firemen retrieved the car, computer programmer John Smith was dead. He was on his way to his sister's wedding.

ENDS

| | | |
|---|---|---|
| 1st sentence – | 21 words | |
| 2nd    ,, | 11 | ,, |
| 3rd    ,, | 9 | ,, |
| TOTAL = | 41 words | |

## ANSWER TO EXERCISE 5

*This is what you should have entered on your Story Lead form:*

WHO    – two sisters aged seven and eight
WHAT   – killed
WHERE  – Talbot Street
WHEN   – last Friday evening
WHY    – don't know, but they were found on a blind bend
HOW    – severe multiple injuries

*This is one 100-word version of the news story:*

Two young sisters died from severe multiple injuries only minutes away from their home. The bodies were found at approximately 5 p.m. last Friday on a blind bend in quiet Talbot Street by resident Mrs Alice Jones.

Seven-year-old Jane Porter and Sarah, eight, went to Mayfield School. They were alone and on their way home when they were killed.

Teachers warn children not to cross at this point but walk to the zebra crossing 100 yards further on. Parents have campaigned for two years to have the crossing moved closer to the school or engage a lollipop lady.

ENDS                              *100 words*

## ANSWER TO EXERCISE 6

Ms Mary Bloggs, Features Editor,
'Everytown News'
24 Bloggs Street, Everytown, NW4 1DE.

Dear Ms Bloggs,

*Feature – £1m for Charity In One Go*

Would you be interested in 1,000 words on a team of six blind people who aim to raise £1m by abseiling down a Fire Brigade practice tower in London – complete with their guide-dogs? The event is planned for 24 June and the funds raised will go to the Institute for the Blind.

The team are in training now and are also finding the sponsors. A number of prominent companies have already promised a total of £897,000.

I will interview each team member, also the managers of the various Workshops for the Blind where the team work. I will also get quotes from the Fire Brigade Chief.

Included in the piece will be interesting statistics from a recent report by the Institute for the Blind on new inventions of home appliances designed for blind people to use. In addition, I will interview the Director of the Institute to discover how he plans to spend the £1m.

I have had several years' experience as a voluntary worker involved with caring for blind people.

As it's only seven weeks to the event, may I look forward to an early reply, please? I enclose a stamped addressed envelope.

Your faithfully

Par 1 – who, what, how, where, when, why, as in a finished news story.
Par 2 – reassurance that £1m isn't an impossible aim.
Par 3 – what quotes will be included,
Par 4 – indicates interesting background info,
Par 5 – shows the author's relevant experience.

The word 'I' kept to the minimum so as not to come over too arrogant.

I didn't need to say I was a journalist, the editor knows that from the succinct, straight-to-the-point, professional style of the outline.

## ANSWER TO EXERCISE 7

PASSIVE: The man was bitten by the dog.
ACTIVE: The dog bit the man.

## ANSWER TO EXERCISE 10

*Suggested headlines:*

ADULT EDUCATION: *'Get Rich in the Schoolroom'*
The angle I chose was learning a skill that can earn money.

LEAD-FREE PETROL: *'Lead-free Turns Your Car Green'*
Angle – all the benefits of lead-free.

HOME COMPUTERS: *'Make your Computer Shop for You'*
Angle – programme your computer to work out a number of weekly shopping lists for a family of four.

Try to think up more of your own.

# ANSWER TO EXERCISE 12

*What are the Four 'Cs'?*

Clothes, Cosmetics, Cookery, Children.

# ANSWER TO EXERCISE 18

Professional-size transparencies (2¼″ × 2¼″) – not 35mm slides.

# ANSWER TO EXERCISE 19

The Silly Season starts in August. It is a period of very little news as Parliament is in recess.

# ANSWER TO EXERCISE 23

Ideas for radio programmes:

*In Touch*
New gardens for the blind; blind people coping with difficult jobs in open industry; novel fund-raising ideas for charities like the National Institute for the Blind and to buy Guide Dogs.

*Does He Take Sugar?*
Volunteer community programmes to arrange for outings for people in wheelchairs; new social clubs to integrate disabled and able people; big achievement by a disabled person either jobwise or in the community.

# Index